Surrealism and the Cinema

Surrealism and the Cinema
(open-eyed screening)

by

MICHAEL GOULD

South Brunswick and New York:
A.S. Barnes and Company
London: The Tantivy Press

©1976 by Michael Gould

A.S. Barnes and Co., Inc.
Cranbury, New Jersey 08512

The Tantivy Press
108 New Bond Street
London W1Y OQX, England

Library of Congress Cataloging in Publication Data

Gould, Michael.
  Surrealism in the cinema.

  Bibliography: p.
  1. Surrealism in motion-pictures. I. Title.
PN1995.9.S85G6   791.43'0909'38   74-9284
ISBN 0-498-01498-3

Cover design by Stefan Dreja

SBN 0-904208-55-9 (U.K.)
PRINTED IN THE UNITED STATES OF AMERICA

"This is not a book."
'Ceci n'est pas un livre.'

oriental laughter
for all my friends
the people I love

Contents

Acknowledgements

In writing this book I asked the assistance of many people. To those who gave freely of themselves I give my deepest thanks:

J.A. Lapointe Films, Montreal, for supplying prints.
Brian Remington, for supplying prints.
Wayne Gartley, for supplying prints.

Brian Kanarenes, for making frame enlargements.
Janis Rothbard, for making frame enlargements.

The Canada Council, for giving me financial assistance in a time of need.

John Locke, for making frame enlargements.
Michael Snow, for supplying prints and stills.
Gerald Pratley for his assistance.

Jay Leyda, for lending his Buddha-like presence.
Lloyd Chesley, for his continuing friendship and creative advice in writing this book.
Jack Horwitz, for making frame enlargements; and for his love.
Paula Fins, for her love.
Jack and Anne Gould, for their endless patience.

André Breton: *Manifestoes of Surrealism,* trans. Richard Seaver and Helen R. Lane (Ann Arbor: University of Michigan Press, 1969). Copyright © 1969 by University of Michigan Press. Courtesy of University of Michigan Press.

The Airconditioned Nightmare, Henry Miller, Copyright 1945 by New Directions Publishing Corporation, Reprinted by permission of New Directions Publishing Corporation, New York, and William Heinemann, Ltd., London.

Mystery and Melancholy of a Street, Giorgio de Chirico, is reproduced by courtesy of Mr. Stanley R. Resor, New Canaan, Connecticut.

Euclidean Walks, René Magritte, is reproduced by courtesy of *The Minneapolis Institute of Arts*.

Surrealism and the Cinema

The Swing, Jean Fragonard, is reproduced by courtesy of *The Wallace Collection*, London.

Western Motel, Edward Hopper, is reproduced by courtesy of Yale University Art Gallery, Bequest of Stephen Carlton Clark.

Film stills by courtesy of The Canadian Film Institute, The British Film Institute, and The Museum of Modern Art Film Stills Archives.

Untitled (Habitat with Owl), Joseph Cornell, is reproduced by courtesy of Doris Starrels, Los Angeles.

Surrealism and the Cinema

1

The Surrealist Sensibility

"Surrealism is within the compass of every consciousness."
                    —Surrealist tract of the Twenties

Before you lies an open book. The title, *Surrealism and the Cinema*,
may lead one to hold certain expectations of this book. One can
assume it is going to be about the cinema, but what can one assume
from this abstract "ism" which creeps more into the consciousness of
people with each passing day?

Although the book contains much material on the films of Luis
Buñuel, there is little space given to the work of other such historically
important surrealist film-makers as Jean Cocteau and René Clair.
Surrealism can be an endless topic, and this is not meant to be a
comprehensive study of "known" surrealist film-makers (a "Ten
Most Wanted" list), nor a review of a movement in cinema. This is just
a selective book about films; a book about art; about perception;
revelation; and appreciation. To expect something else would be a
mistake. If surrealism is anything, it is not what one would expect it to
be; it is something else.

Because film is a new art form, film criticism and study have tended
toward classifying cinema in terms of the other arts. At first it was a
struggle for it to be accepted, by the public and critics alike, as art.
Today that fight has basically been won; but the lack of a lengthy
evolution of critical thought in film has also limited our conception of
film art, and thrown the critic at the mercy of art history, in which the
story of film has only been written for the past seventy-five years. This
limitation is at best a constructive one, for it helps to emphasise the
similarity of all the arts, their oneness; however, it is a limitation that
has tended toward over-simplification. It is the kind of over-
simplification that is responsible for the sensibility that sees "impressionism" in film as merely soft-focus photography and dappled light
patterns, as in the canvases of Renoir—and goes no further; "expressionism" in film, as nightmare worlds of bizarre camera angles and
dark shadows, as in the German Expressionist theatre of Georg

11

Kaiser; and grotesque characters, as in the caricature painting of George Grosz—and goes no further; and "surrealism" in film, as mesmerising montages of shock images (eyeballs and decapitated statues) with a feeling of anarchic defiance and irrational logic (as related to the Surrealist art movement of the Twenties)—and goes no further.

This kind of over-simplification is the criticism of "isms" and pigeon-holes. Where is there room for the explorer? Surrealism is everything for everyone to discover. Jean Cocteau once remarked that all films are surreal. In one sense he was right: Inasfar as they are cultural and psychological fantasies, every film one sees can be read as a dream or desire. This viewpoint is basically that of Parker Tyler. Cocteau, however, may have had something else in mind when he made that statement; that is, that the passing of illuminated images across the screen was for him a surreal experience, an experience that took him beyond his conscious mind. Any film can do this.

The word "experience" will often be used in this text in conjunction with the word "surreal" to emphasise the part subjectivity plays in interpreting this sensibility. Luis Buñuel once remarked that every spectator of his films was welcome to use the pictures as most useful to him.

If Cocteau and Buñuel, in their statements, are concerned with the relatively small world of the cinema, then Salvador Dali, in his statement "Let everyone be able to read from things," shows a more worldly, if not more cosmic, attitude. A true surrealist, who lives out his fantasies in much the same manner as that decadent writer of the late Nineteenth century, Gérard de Nerval; a man who would walk a live lobster on a ribbon about the Jardin du Luxembourg; Dali sees every *thing* as a possible surreal goldmine. The reason for this vast reservoir from which to draw surrealist images and thoughts, is that the domain of surrealism is the human mind, an infinite source of imagination. If surrealism is anything, "It's all in the mind." (Say the Beatles in *Yellow Submarine*) Surrealism is a mind game, one that has influenced the entire history of Twentieth-century art and thought. The people of this century are the people of introspection. They puzzle things out; they think. Some think they think too much; others think they don't think enough; but they all *think* they think something. The art of this century has relentlessly tried to rid itself of superficial, self-imposed content, in order to put the emphasis on this human *perception* of the work of art.

This perception, for the surrealist, is ultimately a sublime notion. It elevates one emotionally. A surreal film (or even a surreal image or moment) takes one out of one's conscious mind into the subconscious. Surrealism effects the emotions *through* the mind. One sees images and makes certian emotional connections in one's mind. If the vision revealed is too much for the rational mind to absorb (too intense, too threatening, too "real") yet cannot be rejected, then it leaves the consciousness and comes to exist on a sublime level as pure surrealism. Two examples come to mind from the films of Buñuel. In *Un chien andalou*, the young man wipes his mouth from his face (!). The woman is annoyed by this act, and checks the hair under her arm. It is gone. She is shocked now to see pubic hair growing like a beard on the man's face, and she defiantly sticks her tongue out at the man, and waves him farewell. A Freudian-symbolic analysis of this sequence would not only be lifelessly pedantic, but also silly. Who really cares about the genital exchange that appears to be represented, or the feelings of sexual insecurity from which this wishy-washy young man suffers? What comes most strikingly across to the viewer is the jocular *manner* in which these two people taunt each other. This is a riotously funny depiction of the battle of the sexes, and because the vision is too bizarre for us to absorb consciously (and a Freudian interpretation of the symbols proves fruitless because it deadens the emotional effect of the sequence) it becomes felt emotionally, as humour in this case, on a

The ecstasy...

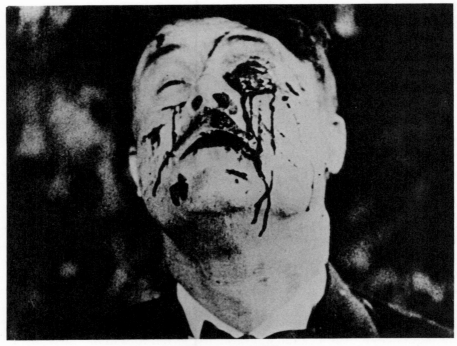

...and the agony of love

subconscious level. It is the *mood* of the sequence that is most important. Symbols, however can be fun, and can be knowingly flaunted. In
The Young One, Buñuel shows a lecherous Zachary Scott with an
apple in his hand, and a young, virginal girl at his side. He tells the
child, "Now you're a *real* woman," and crunches ravenously into the
apple.

Another example, but of a different emotion, occurs in Buñuel's
L'âge d'or. It is the love-death scene in which Lya Lys and Gaston
Modot try desperately to make love to the ironic strains of the Liebes-
tod from Wagner's "Tristan und Isolde." As Modot passionately cries
"Mon amour, mon amour," his mouth and face stream with blood.
The moment is too intense to take consciously. Ecstasy and frustra-
tion, opposing poles of emotional response, are so graphically por-
trayed *together* that it can move us to sublime heights.

André Breton was the Pope of the Surrealist art movement. His
friends called him the Pope, and how apt that name was; if the Pope is
an aloof and pompous figure, so too was Breton. (Surrealists have
always mocked religion, along with all forms of convention, as the
enemy of art.) Beside his poems and novels, his Surrealist Manifestos
may appear as the dictates of a hardened theoretician; one look how-

ever, at a list of things that are surreal for Breton, should open up new
vistas:

> "Swift is Surrealist in malice,
> Sade is Surrealist in sadism.
> Chateaubriand is Surrealist in exoticism.
> Constant is Surrealist in politics.
> Hugo is Surrealist when he isn't stupid.
> Desbordes-Valmore is Surrealist in love.
> Bertrand is Surrealist in the past.
> Rabbe is Surrealist in death.
> Poe is Surrealist in adventure.
> Baudelaire is Surrealist in morality.
> Rimbaud is Surrealist in the way he lived, and elsewhere.
> Mallarme is Surrealist when he is confiding.
> Jarry is Surrealist in absinthe.
> Nouveau is Surrealist in the kiss.
> Saint-Pol-Roux is Surrealist in his use of symbols.
> Fargue is Surrealist in the atmosphere.
> Vaché is Surrealist in me.
> Reverdy is Surrealist at home.
> Saint-Jean-Perse is Surrealist at a distance.
> Roussel is Surrealist as a storyteller.
> Etc.''

In 1913, Marcel Duchamp, probably the greatest mind to exist in the art
world of our century (and also probably one of the silliest) started
making his series of "ready-mades" which were to revolutionise our
entire outlook on art. Such works as *"Bicycle Wheel"*(one wheel from
a bicycle mounted upside-down on a wooden stool, so that one could
spin the wheel) and *"Fountain"* (a porcelain urinal), were not only
attacks on the conservative nature of contemporary art, but a beckon-
ing to people to see art all around them, and to realise that anything is
art if an artist says it is. Some later outgrowths of this sensibility
appeared in happenings; pop art, which saw beauty even in a
Campbell's Soup can; and the use of the artists's own body as his
medium (Vito Acconci, in his *"Trademarks"* (1970), bit himself and
took photographs of the wounds).

Art works stay the same, but art is always changing. The *"Mona
Lisa"*today is not physically much different than when Leonardo

painted it almost five hundred years ago. Perhaps the *petina* has
dulled, and now the painting can only be glimpsed through the reflec-
tions that appear on the glaring glass surface of the protective casing,
but basically it is the same work. It is our perception of the work that
has changed (and must *inevitably* have changed) since the time of the
Italian princes. The *"Mona Lisa"* is no longer just a portrait of a
woman with a certain smile. She has become a deity, to worship or to
attack (Duchamp painted a moustache on his version). One gawks at
her amongst a crowd of pilgrims, curiosity seekers, and cynics, who
gather at the Louvre. She can even metamorphise into a film: while at
the Louvre I was astounded to see a middle-aged Japanese tourist
capturing the painting, complete with the reflection of himself and the
gathered crowd, with his Super-8mm home movie camera.

Duchamp had quite a head for what was to become modern art. He
felt that no work of art was complete unless seen and appreciated by
some spectator (books are written to be read; plays to be seen; and
music to be heard.) The art work cannot exist in a vacuum. The human
mind must bounce off it some thoughts and perceptions to complete
the work of art; and the *"Mona Lisa"* in the Louvre is no more or less a
valid artistic expression than the *"Mona Lisa"* projected at twenty-
four frames per second on some living room wall in Osaka. Duchamp's
idea necessitates the presence of a creative spectator in the absence of
a certain element in all art. That missing element he called the "art
co-efficient," and likened it to the unexpressed but intended, and the
unintentionally expressed. Duchamp saw the artist more as a medium
than a conscious art-maker, who although he may be very aware of
what he is *intending* to do, actually has little control over what the final
results are. The work of art becomes the emotional expression of that
artist's inner state. Sometimes it communicates other things than were
desired (a kind of Freudian slip), and other times it does not express the
things that *were* intended. In the end, the artist cannot interpret his
own work alone. An aesthetic osmosis takes place between the art
work and the spectator, and this is the missing link in all works. The
increasing trend toward audience participation in the theatre reflects
this awareness.

Once we see art as being incomplete until observed, we can then see
that with each new spectator comes a different set of responses.
Similarly, with the coming of advancing periods of history, come new
attitudes toward art. If art is always in the process of metamorphosis,
we can easily accept such changes in values as reflected by the redis-
covery of a van Gogh, or the rejection of a Gerry and the Pacemakers
(for example!). This new awareness puts much responsibility on the

shoulders of the spectator. We can no longer pompously sit and dictate value judgements; that is hardly being a creative participant in the act. It now becomes a matter of love.

"Criticism can only exist as a form of love."

(Breton)

When a critic purports to judge, he has exalted himself to an elevated position over the work of art and the artist. This is not love. Many critics say they love film, and then look down from above. Love is a feeling of oneness and equality with the art work involved, and a loving critic's words are like a rhapsody which inspires others to sing along.

Some of the finest art critism of this century is contained in André Malraux's "Museum without Walls." It is a work that unifies art history under the banner of subjectivity. For Malraux, works of art are not objects that said specific things when they were created, but voices that speak to us now. He shows how human perception of art has changed throughout history; how modern art sees the subject of a work of art not as the "subject" but as the presence of the artist. He writes of how modern photographic methods have altered our awareness of art, with the accessibility of books in which the entire history of art can be seen at a glance: ancient Egyptian on the next page to French Impressionism on the page next to Ming Dynasty. Where, now is the complete art work of the *"Mona Lisa"*? Does it hang in the Louvre or will a good quality photo of the mystical landscapes behind *"La Giaconda"* reveal as much to the viewer as "the real thing"? Are these two representatives of the same vision or are they completely different visions? Malraux sees our perception of art today as being one based on metamorphosis, and we are the first group of people to see art as such.

Film criticism, unfortunately, has yet to produce a Malraux; however, a few critics in touch with this attitude (whether consciously or not, it makes little difference) are Parker Tyler, Raymond Durgnat, and Herman Weinberg. Shocked as they may be to find themselves together on the same page, I believe that they form a brotherhood of rhapsodisers on film and lovers of art. Durgnat's *"Films and Feelings"*, Weinberg's biographies, *"Josef von Sternberg"* and *"The Lubitsch Touch"*, and Tyler's *"Hollywood Hallucination"* and *"Magic and Myth of the Movies"*, are good examples of their work. The critic who insists on objective criticism is not only out of touch with reality, but a fool. These three men are among the most subjectivity-conscious of writers on film. Durgnat emphasises the play of emotions and feelings in film interpretation. He writes that films convey emotions not information, and illustrates this by comparing two stills from Dreyer's *La passion de Jeanne d'Arc*, where Jeanne is seen being interrogated by a different judge in each still. The differences of poses, angles, expressions and tensions all help to relate different sets of emotions, and thereby Durgnat hopes to divest the film of a purely "informatory" content.

Tyler, in his way, does the same with his interpretation, which is very much like Freud's dream interpretation. Films are personal and sociological dreams for Tyler, where there exists not only the surface information, but also the latent content, that is, what one *interprets* from the given information, and what is not necessarily put intentionally on the film. Tyler so divests films of content-intention that his writings rarely mention a director's name. Films, for him, seem to be glowing mirrors that reflect light, sound, and movement, and thereby reflect society. He sees the Hollywood star primarily as the wearer of a mask: Joan Crawford is the eternal "fashion plate"; Gary Cooper the eternal "rustic". Tyler sees things in quotation marks. His interpretations are based on myth-archetypes, he is a searcher of perfect images, the ultimate surrealist venture.

Weinberg's recognition of subjectivity is one of great humility. His books are composed not only of the best of his own thoughts, but also the best of those whom he respects. His books are filled with quotes by artists and philosophers, and a good third of the biographies is donated to interviews and appraisals by other artists who either worked with or knew Weinberg's subjects. In such humble manner Weinberg acknowledges the absurdity of objectivity. In small apologies only does he become more obvious. His prologue to the von Sternberg book contains a quote from Nietzsche: "There are no facts, only interpretations of facts"; and a beautiful little article he wrote for the Canadian film magazine, "Take One", contrasting Bertolucci's *Last Tango in Paris* with Chaplin's *A Woman of Paris*, ends with a gentle nod to the dogmatism of film critics.

The concepts of the oneness of art, and metamorphosis, are important to the surrealist viewpoint. The title of a chapter in the Durgnat book, "Ying Realism, Yang Fantasy" is a good example of this critic's acceptance of duality in film criticism. When writing of Buñuel's *Un chien Andalou*, he raises the issue of whether the film is a poem, because of its symbolic meanings, or a painting, because one can interpret it as a set of pictures. We can see it better now as a film, and our awareness of the other arts can only enhance our awareness of film.

Tyler is the poetic critic, who interprets actors' faces as landscapes, and reflectors of emotions rather than conscious emoters. He writes a chapter on actors' voice qualities (Gary Cooper and Bette Davis are voices from Valley, Mountain and Plain"); the word "metamorphosis" is often used by Tyler; and one chapter in "Magic and Myth of the Movies" deals with schizophrenic tendencies in the roles of certain actors. The comic double-take is seen as a manifestation of split personality, where a character steps out of one self into another; and Hugh Herbert is seen as the classic man who loses his own identity; who when introduced to a room full of people, acknowledges *himself*. This consciousness of duality in Tyler's criticism made him the obvious idol of the outrageous protagonist (Myra-Myron) in Gore Vidal's "Myra Breckinridge".

Metamorphosis is less obviously presented in the writing of Herman Weinberg; however, his knowledge of the classical history of literature, philosophy, music and art makes his writings rich in cultural reverberations. Only Weinberg could write of the two Paris films in one article, commenting pointedly on such diverse subjects as title, tangoes, morality, exuberance of youthful directors, excess and simplicity, and contemporary public response.

The true joyous critic should exalt *in* his art, for he is an artist also. Too often one has the image of a film critic being a theatre-bound anaemic, living in the sheltered world of titillating images. In "Interview Magazine" (March 1973) Tyler talks of living life to its full as a form of art. Weinberg's articles, entitled "Coffee, Brandy and Cigars," lead one to believe that he too may have a touch of the decadent in him. Durgnat likes to dress completely in black.

These critics' prose also reflects this special hedonism. It is rhapsodic. Tyler's is so image-fraught that reading sometimes becomes difficult for the reality-ridden reader; Durgnat can toss in more diverse titles, names, and artistic references in one sentence than anyone; and Weinberg's use of quotations is a song of past values against which he is always measuring and comparing. In a world of content-conscious film criticism, these three men are a constant delight, opening new doorways of vision.

The official surrealist art movement's story has been told often in the history-books and is not a major concern here. Briefly, however, it arose from the ruins of the preceding Dada movement which existed aroung the time of the First World War and shortly after. Dada was a dynamic and aggressive movement and if in retrospect the Dadaists' demonstrations and jokes seem a little silly, they are easily forgiven for the earnestness of their anarchism. Out of this "destructive" movement arose a need not only to destroy old realities but to create new ones. (Of Louis Feuillade's *Les vampires*, Breton wrote: "In *Les vampires* will be found the great reality of the century.") Surrealism arose; an optimistic movement where artists wanted more reality, wanted to go beyond reality.

The surrealist movement was baptised by the Pope (Breton) in the mid-Twenties. Being a poet and a writer, his concerns were more literary than visual, and he and his friends sought to revolutionise thought through a new approach to literature, a more "poetic" approach. As visual artists also progressed from Dada toward surrealism, their influence on the movement took on a firmer grasp, so that today it is the visual artists of the movement who are best remembered.

If the revolutionary consciousness of surrealism can be trace to the anarchism of Dada, surrealism's second side, its hedonism, can be traced to the Symbolists of the late Nineteenth century who sought other worlds beyond concrete events. They desired a world of suggestion, evocation and mood, and the visual interpreters of this sensibility, Gustave Moreau and Odilon Redon, with their mystical-mythical works, along with the more floridly escapist artists of the Art Nouveau movement, share with the following surrealists an almost insatiable desire to go beyond. In literature the mood play of Maurice Maeterlinck. "The Intruder," and the suggestive poetry of Stéphane Mallarmé were expressive of this need.

With the development of the cinema in the Twenties, many of the surrealists saw the ideal medium in which to explore other worlds. Man Ray, Hans Richter and Francis Picabia were among the artists who first experimented with film towards a surreal end. There was some interaction between painters and film-makers, and both Clair and Buñuel started in partnership with official surrealists (Picabia did the script for Clair's *Entr'acte* and Dali was co-writer-director of *Un Chien Andalou*).

By the mid-Thirties surrealism was gathering few new artists to its fold, though the old masters of the movement (Chirico, Dali, Ernst and Ray) continued to progress and expand within their own realms. Most of the experimental surrealist films had already been made, but surrealism was to exert its force over much art to come. As far ahead as the mid-Forties surrealist-inspired dream sequences were to abound in such commercial Hollywood films as *Spellbound* and *Yolanda and the Thief* (a little late, as usual, for that sleepy city). If the surrealist movement *per se* was short-lived, its influence has yet to cease. The movement itself is one thing; the sensibility that started it all and continues to exist is quite another matter.

"When I was a child, I spake as a child, I understood as a child, I thought as a child; but when I became a man, I put away childish things. For now we see through a glass darkly."
                                                        ——1 Corinthians, 13

Surrealism as a sensibility has been and still is concerned with certain ways of perceiving reality, approaching life and art. There are many paths to surrealist consciousness, and they all reflect something of the four basic attitudes: "The Imagistic," "The Conceptual," "The Revelatory" and "The Subjective", all of which are inescapably inter-related. Before dealing with the cinema alone, a more detailed study of these four attitudes will serve to clarify the surrealist sensibility.

The Imagistic. The image is the basic element of surrealism for it is an image-conscious sensibility. For René Magritte, the Belgian painter, the bowler hat is the symbol of the *bourgeois* European man, and Magritte's men in bowlers are all types, without individual personalities. It is the man-in-the-bowler-hat *image* that excites Magritte, and not the man *himself*.

Surrealism concerns itself with a *desire* for the image or object. With the same passionate yearning in which he pursues more reality, the surrealist pursues objects—the more intense they are, the better. The surrealist feels he must become actively involved in the existences of these objects and seeks to form a whole with them. This search becomes so intense that he finds himself catering to a new hunger, and suffers from a want of fulfilment. He desires to devour the images about him, to ravish the world of its images. As Dali has written, this desire to become one with the object eventually leads to the ultimate fusion: a desire "to *eat* the object." It is no surprise that Dali has recently issued a cook-book, lavishly illustrated with photo-montages and dazzling pictures of elaborately decorated examples of French cuisine. When a surrealist sits down to dinner he is feasting on the ideal images of his dreams. Peter Kubelka has added cooking to film-making as a form for his artistic expression, the only one in which one can actually fuse with the object of one's own creation. One can see the materialistic tendencies of surrealism here. It may be a sensibility that aims at a revolution of thought, but this is not necessarily at odds with the hedonistic side of its split personality.

The actual appearance of eatable objects in surrealist works is further evidence of this concern. Milk, bread and fried eggs have been featured in Dali's work; and in the Sixties Claes Oldenburg was creating such delicacies as his giant plastic hamburger.

As Dali has written, the object goes through four stages: At first it exists outside one; then it transforms itself into the shape of one's desire and acts upon one's contemplation; it can be acted upon; and finally, the object makes one pursue a fusion with it. The quest to merge with object-images leads inevitably to desiring *ideal* objects. The insatiability of the surrealist will not let him be of a passive frame of mind; constantly in search of the truth, his pursuit continues until perfection has been achieved (if that is possible). This ideal for which the surrealist searches is the Platonic Ideal, and it is always the ultimate illustration of the concept an object embodies. For Dali, as for many surrealists, the *Art Nouveau* architecture was an example of images fulfilled, of desires grown solid. These structures show such disdain for reality and such a yearning for shelter in an idealised world. The ultimate surrealist structure (and how apt it should be a church) is Antonio Gaudi's "*Sagrada Familia*" in Barcelona—a study in pure escapism. The church's construction spanned Gaudi's lifetime and is yet to be finished (begun in 1887); yet it still feels like a complete vision of ideal escapist pursuit.

Looking at the front facade one can see the development over the years, from the French Gothic style in which the base was started, with its three gabled portals, to the decoration surrounding it, which metamorphoses into the *Art Nouveau's* flowing leaf patterns, to the towers, which are like tall, honey-combed candles and are without precedent in style; to the pinnacles, which are cubist. This is the work of a man constantly searching for ideal styles and changing his work as it progresses. At first sight the building looks like a wedding cake that is becoming mushy at the bottom, or the vision of a schizophrenic sand-castle builder. Gaudi was a fervent Catholic, and the church was built in a truly religious spirit for his idealised world.

Similar to the idea of image-idealisation is the concept of image-intensity. The intensity of the plastic image of an object is responsible for the degree of its influence upon our consciousness. The ''shot'' has often been proclaimed as the basic element of film. In a technical-practical sense this is right, for a shot is something concrete with which the director and crew can work. When making a film, all the creative energy at the time of filming is concentrated on making the shot; however, in the surrealist film experience, the presence of the image (representing an idea) is more influential on our awareness than the shot itself. An image can only be contained by one shot, but a single shot can contain many distinct images. An image consists of a perception of a moment in film where every element comes together to say one thing to a viewer; it becomes a complete reality; and the more elements that reinforce the purity of that moment, the more intense the emotional effect. In Alfred Hitchcock's *Rear Window* the camera roams around the inner courtyard of James Stewart's apartment complex in a few shots; but the images shown to the spectator are more numerous, as they appear in the vignettes of human activity and passions that are glimpsed through the windows that border the courtyard. It is the various images of these people's lives that stick in our mind, even more so than the voyeuristic nature of the camera movements and the shots. Hitchcock is showing us more than images of people; he is showing people as types; and his window-frame vision on their lives enhances the role-like quality of their existences. Each life has its own representative action, so that throughout the film we know basically what kind of action each character will perform: the busty beauty with the men admirers; the young newly-weds in their underwear and love-making; the elderly couple clutching their pet dog; the struggling composer at his piano, straining for the final chords to complete his concerto of the city; and Miss Lonelyhearts, with her matronly dress and tacky apartment. Hitchcock, like Magritte, is not interested in the individual, but in the archetype; and it is through the various techniques of film that he can manipulate our responses to his images; however, as programmed and tightly constructed as an image may be, it is still a more difficult thing for a director to control than a shot. A shot is concrete, with beginning and end boundaries; an image is more abstract, and though a director may try for a specific emotional response to any image, we must not forget that "image" and "imagination" come from the same root. The mind's contemplation of the image reflects the second attitude of surrealism.

The Conceptual. As children we are given our first taste of surrealism at the cinema. Having been ushered into dark theatres, we have all participated in the barrage of luminous images that passed across the screen. It is only children, or the child-like in spirit, who are capable of feeling for the hidden reaches of surrealism. That the forest fire in *Bambi* or the wicked witch in *Snow White and the Seven Dwarfs* could haunt the dreams of so many for so long is an affirmation, not only of the intense emotional state of the child-like, but of the part the imagination plays in interpreting art with an elaborate set of emotional responses.

The imagination, and its function in art, is a two-fold thing. The artist needs imagination to conceive something from nothing, and the spectator needs imagination in order to interpret the art and make it a concrete experience. If being creative is to be perceptive, then being perceptive is also a creative activity. The surrealist bases his reality on the validity of the observations and constructions of his own imagination; and by doing so, places a great importance on the conceptual abilities of the mind.

This emphasis on the mind should not lead one to think of surrealism in terms of rationalism, for surrealists are only interested in the irrational, game-like nature of the mind. Breton resurrected a statement from a writer of the late Nineteenth century, Comte de Lautréamont, to serve as the complete expression of the surrealist sensibility:

"Beautiful, like the chance meeting of a sewing machine and an umbrella on a dissecting table."

This statement illustrates the concept of the irrational juxtaposition of objects so crucial to an understading of surrealism. What do a sewing machine, an umbrella and a dissecting table have in common? Nothing. Here, however, one finds them in the same world; the worlds of the seamstress, the thunderstorm and the scientist, all quite rational on their own, are brought together, perfectly by chance, to exist in a not quite comfortable oneness—and it is beautiful. Different worlds are of interest to the surrealist only when seen together, for it is the dissimilarity and contrast of the worlds that cause the reverberations in the mind. Because the surrealist endows the object with such powers of persuasion, that two opposing or non-related realities could even exist side by side is a sign of audacity.

Henry Miller, an astute spectator of the surrealist cinema, writes in his book, *"The Airconditioned Nightmare,"* upon seeing a shop window with a nylon stocking display, "Thus we see how Surrealism penetrates to every nook and corner of the world." Miller finds shop windows surreal, not only because early surrealists used mannequins and doll *motifs* in their work, but more because of the presence of two distinct and intense realities existing together. The presence of the window, a quiet world meticulously created from props and lights, is set, with a frame around it, on a public street, where the reality of people shuffling by in their everyday existences is present. It is this juxtaposition that sparks an awareness of absurdity on some level, whether it is the quiet-shuffling duality of the relationship that excites Miller, or the artificial-natural quality, or whatever. There is room for the mind to ramble and find one's own awareness of the absurd here.

The paintings of Paul Delvaux are a good example of this concept of the irrational juxtaposition of objects. Many of his works are landscapes in which some figure (usually a woman) rests. A woman may be seen reposing in a bedroom, yet outside the back window of the room, a steam locomotive is seen coming on a path directly toward the room. What is this train *doing* here?! René Magritte also exploits this irrational logic. He has done large paintings of rooms, where a barren interior is totally filled by the presence of one object; in one work it is a green apple, in another a luscious red rose. *How* did they get there? *Who* put them there? These questions, which make the viewer react toward the work of art with a kind of comic double-take, are part of the untold mind games the surrealist poses to himself when confronted with an irrational piece.

Putting unrelated objects together is only one way of irrational juxtaposition. In *Un chien andalou* a hand is seen ringing a doorbell and the following shot is one of two hands coming through cut-out holes in a wall, shaking a cocktail shaker vigorously. Here the relationship is also absurd on its *sound* level; all the more incredible given the fact that this is a silent film. Buñuel credits his audience with much intelligence, for in this brief moment of film time one must make the mental change from "ding" to "shake-rattle," and see the contrast and humour of it.

Surrealism cannot exist without this gamesmanship. It is so totally without reason and so filled with fun that it is appealing to the absurdist nature of the surrealist. Breton composed many games to be played by his friends, with titles such as "How not to be bored any longer when with others," " To write false novels" and "How to catch the eye of a woman you pass in the street." This third game consists of five rows the width of the page of a book, of black type dots (periods)! Dali also

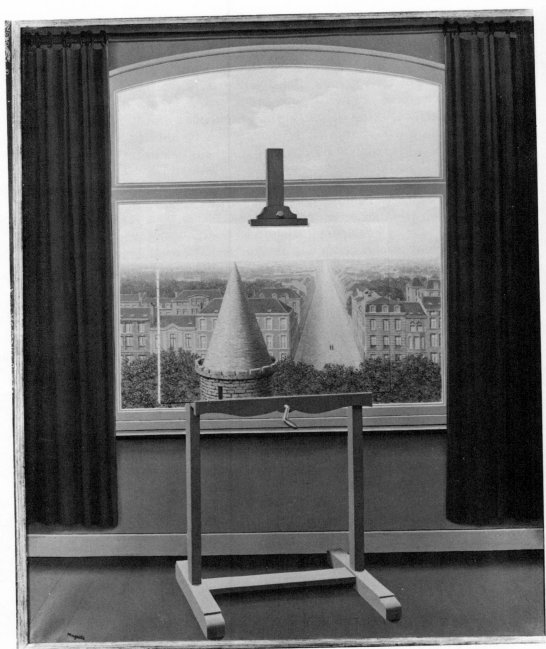

"Euclidean Walks," by René Magritte (reproduced by courtesy of the
Minneapolis Institute of Arts)

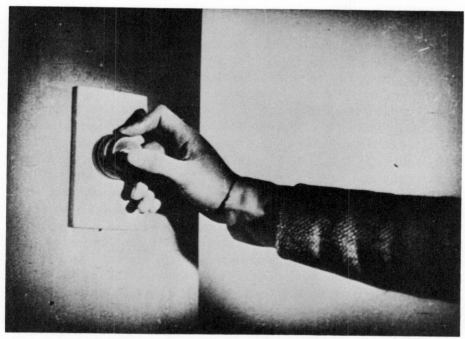

Above and below: UN CHIEN ANDALOU

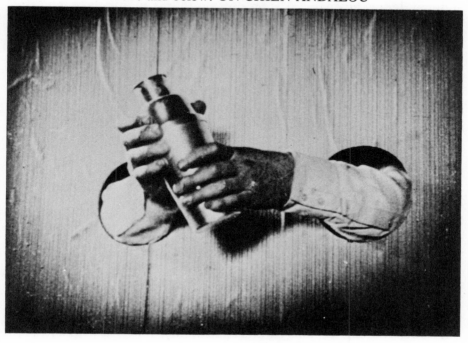

delights in creating games; any interview with him is filled with circuit-ous turns of language and logic so as to taunt, confuse and entice the listener.

Trompe l'oeil is a mind-game *genre* of painting that deals in "fooling the eye." Basically, all realistic painting does this, for the artist is attempting to portray three-dimensional objects on a two-dimensional surface, and must use the tricks of perspective to help him; but this term was more specifically used to describe certain American paint-ings of the Nineteenth century in which artists (like Peto and Harnett) attempted realistically, to portray flat surfaces like walls, bookshelves and cupboards, which had been encrusted with paper tackings, memorabilia and hanging objects. Harnett did four versions called *"After the Hunt,"* in which a wooden door was shown cluttered with relevant objects: a rifle, a hunting horn, some dead pheasants and hares strung up, etc. There was a certain preciousness in the subject-matter, and an orderliness and neatness to its handling; a stillness existed, and the concern to push *trompe l'oeil* to its limits. That is to say, that by severely limiting the depth factor in a painting (in *"After the Hunt"* the depth covered amounts to about eight inches) and keeping the painted objects equivalent in size to their actual size, the artist could trick the viewer into making him see the painted object as "the real thing." All the devices of perspective are here stretched over a minimal depth; however, it is an illusion that is momentary, and the viewer's excitement in viewing a *trompe l'oeil* painting comes from his realization that his *oeil* has been *trompe*'d.

Trompe l'oeil is a demonstrative and revelatory *genre*. Everyday objects are pictured in such detail as to "point out" to the viewer the inner truth of the objects (and this is the quality of all still life). The surrealist wants not only that questions should be raised regarding the irrational, but also that things be *revealed* to him in fresh and marvel-lous manner.

> "What men or gods are these? What maidens loth?
> What mad pursuit? What struggle to escape?
> What pipes and timbrels? What wild ecstasy?"
> —Keats "Ode on a Grecian Urn"

The Revelatory. Looking back upon Lautréamont's quote, one notices that he put beauty first; but of what nature is it? For Breton, "Only the marvellous is beautiful." Surrealism, in its constant search, seeks always the experience that will be revelatory; that will dazzle one with new delights. This calls for a child-like ability at wonderment.

THE SCARLET EMPRESS

Children are so easily surprised because they have so little experience in life; but the adult surrealist has had a surplus of exposure to people and media; and it is by an act of supreme will that the surrealist can see things as a child.

In her excellent book on the German Expressionist cinema, "The Haunted Screen," Lotte Eisner elaborates upon the expressionist actor, illustrating her point with shots of actors in moments of frenzied hysteria. She recalls the comment by Kasimir Edschmid (a theorist of expressionism in the early years of this century) who wrote that "the expressionist man wears his heart painted on his sleeve." Her examples illustrate her point well, for the expressionist world is one of surface emotions and passions. If one could find a "Surrealist Look" it might be the expression of the face of Marlene Dietrich, in *The Scarlet Empress,* where she watches a hole being driven through the eye of an ikon on her chamber wall by a long drill (Sam Jaffe, as the mad prince, is the culprit). Her head, tilted a little to one side, her lips slightly ajar, her eyes round with astonishment, Dietrich expresses the look of surprise *par excellence.* The drilling shot itself, is the most baroque moment in this very baroque film: a swirling line traces a path that cuts across simple screen time and space. The cock of Dietrich's head initiates the circular movement; a cut to what she is watching reveals a long drill, spiralling forward toward the viewer, piercing the eye of the ikon. (Eyes seem to often be associated with spiral formations. In Hitchcock's *Psycho*, the shower-murder scene ends with a shot of water spiralling into the round drain, and the next scene dissolves to an extreme close-up of the eye of the fallen victim, as the camera retreats in a spiralling movement.) If Dietrich is astonished at what she sees, the spectator of the film can be equally astonished by the movement and beauty of these images. One watches a surreal film with the same expression with which Dietrich watched the drilling, thinking "I can't believe it; but I do."

Being shown a secret truth or beauty is at the heart of the revelation of the marvellous for the surrealist. One wants miracles to happen. Louis Aragon, the surrealist writer, wrote: "What characterises the miracle, proclaims the miraculous, that quality of the marvellous, is undoubtedly a bit of surprise. . . " "Surprise" can be a misleading word, if one relates it to Hitchcock's concept of the word as the opposite of "suspense." For him, suspense requires a prolonged emotional response based on mystery, and surprise is an immediate emotional response to a sudden revelation. Surprise, in the surrealist sense, does put emphasis on the immediacy of the emotion and the importance of sudden revelation, for it is interested in shock and astonishment; yet it goes deeper than that. Surprise is the *spice* of life (the surrealist takes his food hot) and surrealism seeks more the *newness* that surprise has to offer than the immediate emotional release. The surrealist is jaded, and surprise offers him something previously unknown or inexperienced. It offers one a new truth, and in doing so the revelation of the marvellous can be seen as a religious concept. With this new information it is not surprising (or perhaps it *is* surprising) to discover surrealist resonances in two films of religious revelation: Cecil B. DeMille's *The Ten Commandments* and George Stevens's *The Greatest Story Ever Told*. A study of these films will help to clarify the nature of the questions raised by irrational juxtaposition, and the "answers" put forth by the revelation of the marvellous.

If at first thought one is struck by the Hollywood commercialism of these films and refuses to let in any further influences to aid seeing them as valid expressions of religious intent, one has only to consider the two men who *made* these works; and "made" is precisely the word. Studio system interference included, the work and devotion these directors put into their films justifies calling them true creators. Both films appear at the end of the *oeuvres* of the respective directors. *The Ten Commandments* was DeMille's last film before he died. He had made a silent version, but wished to recreate, on a larger scale, this most cherished property. Stevens made only one film thereafter — *The Only Game in Town*. Both biblical films stand as summations of their creators' lifeworks. For DeMille, it was his largest and greatest show; for Stevens, it was the culmination of his work in the Fifties, when he was achieving his true blossoming as a romanticist, by exploring the epic nature of film, through leisurely pacing, extending action through prolonged montage and slow dissolves. In this way, *The Greatest Story Ever Told* is the natural climax to his preceding *Shane* and *Giant*. Stevens's return to a more slight *genre,* in the comic drama of *The Only Game in Town*, represents a complete reversal of style, reflecting his own awareness that he had taken one theme to its obvious conclusion, and once that had been accomplished, he had nowhere else to go but to return to his earlier interests of the Thirties, which his final film so aptly captures.

That these films were so spiritually important to the men who made them (and most artists' final works, if done at a mature age, reflect a religious concern)is reflected in how seriously they took their projects. DeMille's film was something like five years in the making (if one is to believe the publicity), and the Stevens film was about three years in the making. The sheer intensity of concentration these men must have sustained over those years is sign enough of the sincerity of their visions. With DeMille (the Poussin of the cinema-both artists having a certain awkwardness in capturing naturalistic human gestures) it is the showman's vision. He tries to astound his audience and to reveal his truths (banal sentiments though they be, there lies the wit of DeMille) with all the audacity of a magician. His vision raises few questions but provides many answers, presented in lightning—bolts of truth. During the four hours of *The Ten Commandments*, we witness the various plagues brought by Moses: some impress us, others have been seen before; and it depends on the gullibility of the spectator as to how much he is impressed. But who has ever seen the Red Sea actually part? (Unless one was a witness of DeMille's earlier recreation of this event.) The mid-Fifties back-projection is obvious and clumsy, yet there still remains the sight of the multitudes of Israel walking amidst walls of tumultuously-moving water. Is there a film-maker around who would dare to do this type of scene again, and with such a straight face? DeMille interprets the Bible so literally that his film becomes a fantastical tale of miracles.

After talking with the burning bush, Moses comes down from Mount Sinai with a longer beard than when he first ascended, and surrounded by an unearthly glow. Here we are witness to the results of revelation on Moses; and throughout the film, as his dialogues with God increase,

THE TEN COMMANDMENTS

his beard continues to metamorphose, becoming longer and whiter.

DeMille also has a certain audacity when it comes to his script. Besides giving lengthy credit to many religious books as source material (in an attempt to lend a respectable authenticity to what the intelligent viewer knows to be pure fantasy), DeMille has a knack for turning a phrase that astounds one with its brazen simplicity. Moses, the master-builder of cities erected to glorify Pharaoh, presents a new city and its most prominent monument to Pharaoh, exclaiming, "Here is the obelisk of your Jubilee." With monumental panache, DeMille treats two distinct words with the same kind of respect that a public school teacher lavishes on the two or three difficult words in the daily lesson of a Grade Five speller.

De Mille is at his most astonishing when he makes his audience confront God. To how many films can one go and literally *hear* the voice of God? Not only do we hear His majestic voice, but we see His lightning fingers streak from heaven and carve the commandments into the side of a cliff. As simplistic and comic-bookish as his vision is, it is a unique and revelatory one.

If DeMille lets us hear God, Stevens actually has the courage to *show* him—Max von Sydow truly *is* the Son of God. Unlike DeMille, Stevens is a very quiet man, who, when on the set of a film, will hold up production for a few moments of silent meditation upon a problem of production. His quiet and reflective nature are mirrored by his devotion to spending years in the editing room, where in silence, he alone can make the creative decisions that mould his films. This sensitive side of Stevens combines with his sincerity and belief in the "Truth as Truth," to present a religious vision that may be literal and simple, but being created in love and devotion, is rich in those qualities, and not simplistic and brassy as in DeMille's vision.

By "Truth as Truth" is meant the validity of the *cliché* as truth. All *cliché*s are true, that is why they are *cliché*s. To resurrect the emotional truth behind the *cliché* is a difficult job, but when accomplished, as by Stevens, it becomes a magnificent feat. In film, Shakespeare and the Bible present the greatest problems in making "straight" versions while still maintaining a freshness (for the western viewer). There have been so many varied interpretations of Shakespeare, in attempts to restore life to lines heard so often. As for the sayings of the Bible, and the truths they contain, these pose the same problems. Stevens very obviously believes the truth contained in the St. James version, and with stark simplicity he presents the life of Christ to the spectator as a series of events, following the parables, unfolding the stories as in a child's story book, with miracles and revelations presented as such, for all to wonder at. Carl Sandburg is given a credit for creative participation, and we can see the similarity between these two men as visionaries of simplicity and purity.

The *cliché* as truth is one of the most intense realities with which an artist can deal (relying as it does on shared cultural preconceptions), and one that is not often touched upon, for the obvious fear of failing to transcend the *cliché* and remain emotionally lifeless.

The irrational raises its unlikely head continuously in *The Greatest Story Ever Told*. What is John Ford's Monument Valley doing in Bibleland? Stevens has set many exteriors amidst the splendid buttes of Utah; and the awareness on the spectator's part of the role these monuments played in previous films can only create an absurd relationship in one's mind. Western resonances are felt, and the American myth of the loner who's "gotta do what a man's gotta do" comes to mind. The parallel with Christ as anti-hero is astonishing; and to realise the existence of these two realities together on the same screen (two

STAGECOACH (1939). The familiar Western landscape...

images of reality subliminally felt) is to see the surrealist irrational juxtaposition.

Equally mystifying is the casting of the film. Every major star in Hollywood at that time seems to be present. One might think, "Not another all-star extravaganza?" Charlton Heston is John the Baptist; John Wayne plays a centurion, Shelley Winters is a "woman of no name"; Claude Rains is Herod; Pat Boone is the young man at the tomb, Carroll Baker; Dorothy McGuire; Victor Buono; and so on.

Stevens, however, seems purposely to have chosen these stars for the archetypal natures of their screen *personae*. It is a tribute to Stevens's humility that we never become aware of the egocentricity of any performer. Every actor transcends the commercially-bound facet of his or her personality and comes to embody the single *persona* for which they are individually best suited. Heston, the heroic leader in many an historical picture, plays the Baptist as pure power; John Wayne, in probably the smallest part of his career, plays a centurion, reinforcing his nature as "the lawman"; Claude Rains as Herod is not very far from the corrupt senator in Capra's *Mr. Smith Goes To Washington*; Pat Boone's boyish-faced image is used momentarily as a symbol and reflector of purity. No single player is on screen very long, with the exception of von Sydow as the Son of God, but Stevens uses

...becomes populated with strange inhabitants (THE GREATEST STORY EVER TOLD)

the images projected by their careers to enforce his points. Von Sydow, then virtually unknown in America, plays Christ with the same severe purity as the men he played for Bergman. The contrast between his "new" face and the known faces of all the other characters in the film, enforces the spectator's faith and credence in His word. The film is a miracle of casting, at the very least.

How Stevens is constantly shattering our expectations is his way of raising questions. What is Monument Valley doing here? How can a film with so many familiar faces expect to be fresh?

A further irrational juxtaposition is displayed in the look of the film. Despite the location shooting and great detail to the naturalism of the sets, costumes and actions, there exists in the film a strong feeling for the poetic. People in groups are seen in highly-stylised compositions; glass shots are used; and incredible helicopter shots that careen over a desert landscape end on the Baptist performing his ritual in a river bed. Through Stevens's most langorous editing, sequences are extended for poetic effect. Sal Mineo, the cripple, walks; and Stevens cuts back and forth between his legs and joyous face more times than is really necessary to simply establish the fact. The rising of Lazarus from the grave is an extended sequence of people running throughout the village, spreading the word, to the joyous chords of Handel's "Hallelujah

Chorus.'' Stevens also has many transitional sequences of long lines of people trekking through the desert, with lengthy lap dissolves. The entire film, in fact, is a study in *montage*, with *mise-en-scène's* function being reduced to a minimum, for emotional effect. Rather than conflicting with the reality of religious simplicity as presented in the film, this poetic lyricism and technical virtuosity exists in a harmonious discord with it, and provokes and astounds the spectator.

Stevens's answers to our questions are straightforward; but we must remember that he is a man who believes in the truth of the *cliché*. Most films in which Christ appears treat their subject either too gingerly (where we see only the back side or hand of Christ, as in *Ben-Hur*) or very commonly (as the "everyman" figure in Pasolini's *The Gospel according to Saint Matthew*). Stevens presents the viewer with a full-frontal attitude: von Sydow *is* the son of God. When Christ tells a group of men, "He that is without sin among you, let him first cast the stone," it is an old phrase so starkly uttered that it is endowed with new meaning. Every truth, as presented in this film, is pronounced with the same, simple, serious intent. There exists an openness in Stevens's attitude with which he confronts his audience, and it is this quiet level of the film, when seen simultaneously with the epic grandeur of the film, that astounds the spectator and helps to reveal the truth of Christ.

Giorgio de Chirico, the Italian surrealist painter, wrote about revelation in art; and developed his ideas from the following statement by Schopenhauer, in the latter's "Parerga und Paralipomena": "To have original, extraordinary, and perhaps even immortal ideas, one has but to isolate oneself from the world for a few moments so completely that the most commonplace happenings appear to be new and unfamiliar, and in this way reveal their true essence." Chirico further stated that if one imagines the birth of a work of art in an artist's mind, one will grasp the principle of revelation in art, and the revelation of a work of art reveals the joy of creation. A more subjective approach to art could not be imagined.

The Schopenhauer statement inadvertently exists as a perfect description of a drug experience. Drugs, used frequently by many surrealists, transport the subject to fresher, more child-like states of emotional awareness. They can be taken by the artist as a stimulus to hallucinate, an activity the surrealist uses from which to draw his ideas. Dali once constructed a special pair of amber-coloured sunglasses. Instead of single-glass lenses, he had thin chambers filled with live insects. One can easily see how a few moments' vision through these spectacles could show things never previously imagined.

The Subjective. Thinking back to Breton's list of what is surreal for him, reminds us of the subjective nature of this sensibility. Dali writes that it is possible "to systematise confusion thanks to a paranoiac and active process of thought, and so assist in discrediting completely the world of reality." Once our old attitudes to the reality around us are removed, the comforting pablum of their presence is also gone, leaving us with new fears, which appear in the form of a lack of definitive answers (a fear of the unknown). It is with his own subject-being that the surrealist tries to fill that void, and to be the medium and missing link with art.

This presence of the artist as subject is what Malraux saw as Twentieth century man's attitude toward art. Chirico wrote that art should be stripped of all subject matter in favour of an aesthetic-synthesis, where man as *guide* should be suppressed in favour of seeing man, and everything else, as *thing*. The rational consciousness of the artist as "author" has been further reduced with the introduction of "automatic writing" by Breton, and its visual equivalent, "frottage," by Max Ernst. These techniques sought to free the subconscious and exonerate the author from any hand in his creations. Breton's writing method emphasised spontaneously writing down the first things that came into one's head, without regard to preconceived notions or thought-censorship; and Ernst's technique developed from his first soft pencil rubbings of rough, wooden floor-boards. The patterns he captured stimulated his hallucinatory nature, helped him to elaborate on the patterns, and relieved him of a thoroughly conscious intention.

In film criticism, still somewhat alone amongst the arts, there exists a rejection or unwillingness to accept this subjective view of art. In fictional film, the characters' actions are still regarded as the subject matter; in documentary cinema, the event or person being filmed is still the subject-matter. It is only in the realm of "abstract experimental" film that criticism has accepted the rejection of subject-matter in favour of the presence of the artist. These films are seen to contain many *things* (colour, movement, spatial relationships, etc.) that combine to give the total experience of the film. This kind of interpretation seems proper when applied to abstract film-making, but why should it not be just as appropriate when used with fictional or documentary film? It can be, but only when the viewer realises that it can.

"We shall be idealists subscribing to no ideal. The ideal images of
surrealism will serve the imminent crisis of consciousness; they will
serve Revolution."

—Dali

Because surrealism makes the mind puzzle and search, it is basically
a constructive sensibility, which is bent on tearing down old values and
opening up new horizons; and as such, it is a political sensibility. At the
opening of Buñuel's *L'âge d'or* in Paris, a manifesto, written by most
of the surrealist artists of the time, was circulated. In it, was laid down
the basic attack of surrealism; an assault on the complacency of human
values, as manifested in our capitalistic and religion-oriented society.
The surrealists suggested that one thing alone could transcend everything else: love. Although the surrealists have been depicted as anarch-
ists, demonstrators, hallucinators and irrationalists, it is as the proc-
laimers of love that they are their most representative, and in their
manifesto they appear as the precursors of the romantic, early Beatles,
in their proclamation for "Love, love, love, love."

The surrealist film experience arises from an intense emotional
response to two major approaches to film-making. The first is the
irrational approach, which relies either on the beauty of the unexpected in any way it may reveal itself, or on the irrational juxtaposition
of objects. Of the former type, the emotion can be funny and absurd
(like the mountain goat slipping off the cliff in Bunuel's *Terre sans
pain*); or it can be grotesque and shocking (like the eyeball-slitting
scene in *Un chien andalou*, or the attack on the legless cripple in *Los
olvidados*). The emotion, however, is never rooted in logic. This is a
world where there are no rules and no preconceptions. It is the world of
the anarchist. The irrational juxtaposition of objects is the filmic equivalent of Magritte's logic. *Brats*, an early Laurel and Hardy sound
short, concerns Stan and Ollie as obnoxious children of six. All the
furniture and props are proportionately bigger than they are, and the
entire comedy of the film comes from the visual conflict of sizes and
the absurdity of it.

The second major approach is the exaggerated one. Though it too
stems from the irrational, it relies mostly on the co-existence of an
extremely exaggerated element with some element of reality. The
exaggerated quality is more influential than the actual juxtaposition,
because it reaches an ultimate level: the Platonic Ideal. Ultimate aims
represent the desire for perfection, for the ideal form or ideal situation;
and carrying things to their extreme, while maintaining some foothold
on the "real" world (whether by use of plot, character, location, etc.)
becomes a surrealistic film experience.

Disney's *Snow White and the Seven Dwarfs* and *Pinocchio* contain

PINOCCHIO. Even in black-and-white the Blue Fairy radiates her essence.
Copyright © Walt Disney Productions

elements of the Platonic Ideal which become surreal. In the former
film, the witch's poison apple, so perfectly formed (it is a Delicious
apple) and so startlingly red, is the Platonic Ideal—the very
archetype—of the word "apple." In the latter film, the Blue Fairy
visits Pinocchio. She radiates a golden-blue glow, and has the most
delicately white complexion that ever existed on a screen. She is even
a more perfect illustration of "beauty" than Josette Day in Cocteau's
Beauty and the Beast; and although Disney was only intending to
conjure images of childhood fantasy with the utmost precision, that
does not prevent one from experiencing these images as surreal. How
far is Disney's interpretation from Cocteau's written introduction to
his fairy tale film, dedicated to the wondrous world of the child? Does it
matter which artist is really more or less aware of the surreal implica-
tions of his art? As Herman Weinberg has shown in his book, "Josef
von Sternberg," the shot of the snowbound train, almost engulfed in
white, in *The Devil Is a Woman*, is the "ne plus ultra" of being
snowbound. It is the Platonic Ideal and it inspires in the viewer an
emotion of sublime intensity upon having glimpsed perfection.

Rouben Mamoulian's *Blood and Sand* is the most sustained example
of how exaggerated colour can be used to create a surreal film experi-

ence. This is a film where the emotional burden is carried, not by the characters or the action, but primarily by the colours used, and their intensity. The film's story concerns the rise to fame of an arrogant young man as a great matador; his love for his pure childhood sweetheart, whom he marries, his flirtation with a woman of sin, his fall from grace, retribution and death in the arena. Throughout the film Mamoulian attempts to reach his audience's emotions (and to counteract the nullifying quality of the dull script) through portions of comic relief, the use of evocative guitar music, and other *frissons*; but it is so obvious from the start that it is specifically the colour of the film which most interests Mamoulian, and which is so graphically conveyed to the spectator.

The early Forties (when this film was made) saw the Technicolor process reach the zenith of its intensity. Gone are the light, pastel shades of the early Thirties, and replacing them are colours of such richness as to dazzle the eye. At that time the red, green and blue negatives that combine to give the colour spectrum were all filmed on separate stock, so that in the final processing each colour could be individually controlled, without impinging on the values of other colours (unlike today, when all the colour negatives are combined on one piece of film stock). Mamoulian combined the inherent intensity of his colour process with his own unique vision of the psychological effect of colour, to produce a film that really does not speak unless seen in colour. For example, after introductory sequences of the protagonist as a boy, time passes, and our next look at him occurs when he has matured into a budding matador. Inside a train car, some of his friends are talking to him as he reads hidden behind a newspaper. They ask him a question. Mamoulian then cuts to a close shot of the paper, which is suddenly flipped down to reveal the arrogantly beautiful face of Tyrone Power (our first sight of him). His head rests on a crimson cushion; its colour so pure and intense that its likes have rarely been seen. With the flood of this colour on the screen, our emotions are struck by the character's brazen egocentricity; though as good an actor as Tyrone Power is, it is the scarlet passion of the cushion that acts as a punch to the viewer and conveys the emotion. In black-and-white this emotional kick would just not exist. This is not the *decorative* use of colour (as in most of Minnelli's films), nor the *symbolic* use of colour (as in Antonioni's *The Red Desert*) in which one equates certain colours with certain traits (red equals passion; blue equals tranquility) and links them to characteristics of the people in the film. In *Blood and Sand* the use of colour *is* symbolic, in that the red cushion objectively tells us that the man who rests his head upon it is a vain and passionate

A spotlight helps to intensify the shocking pink dress

person, but it simultaneously is used *emotionally*, and also acts upon the spectator as a visual stimulus.

Like some films which are built on musical *motifs* or recurring images, *Blood and Sand* is built on *motifs* of colour. Red (the unique "red" of this film should really be given another name) is the most dominant one. Symbolically, it is not only used to show the protagonist's arrogance, but it is appropriated by the lustful woman (Rita Hayworth) who seduces Power. We first catch sight of her in the darkened chapel; she wears a purple dress, with red hair, red lipstick and red fingernails. Later in the film her fingers caress the strings of a guitar, but now the use of colour becomes more emotional, as the camera lingers on this action in close-up, letting her fingers caress the spectator with equal passion. A rendez-vous between the two lovers finds them sitting at opposite sides of a chess table. He has the white men and she the hallucinatory red men. There is little dialogue in this scene, for any additional attempt at clarifying their relationship, beyond this colour metaphor, would be superfluous. Again, this could be interpreted as more symbolic than emotional, but in a later scene, when Hayworth rejects Power for a new rising star (Anthony Quinn) she flings off her full-length black cape, vampire-style, to reveal a shocking pink gown, in a moment that is emotionally stupefying for the spectator; insolence, in the guise of pure colour, has been unleashed upon the spectator.

Red is also associated with others at the more passionate moments in the film. At one point, Linda Darnell, as the (usually) white-clothed wife, touches the red handle of her husband's sword, reflecting not only her own fear of his death in the arena, but also intensifying the audience's anticipation of that final event. It inevitably occurs, and the last shot of the film pans past the victorious new matador (Quinn) to the sand of the arena, littered with flowers, hats, and the red blood stain of the fallen hero. The shade has become wine-coloured, as it recedes into the sand, and the viewer's emotions come to rest. Red had carried the spectator from passion, abuse and fear to acceptance.

An astounding attempt to intensity colour occurs in the dining room scene at the vamp's mansion. All the colour has been virtually eliminated through painting the set in blacks, whites and greys, and spraying-down the set to dull the tones, The previous scene had been one of intense colour and an emotional high-point in the film, and Mamoulian wanted to create a colour-emotional low-point, which would act as a transition for the following scene, again one of high colour-emotion (the chess table scene). With this device Mamoulian endows the film with an emotional *rhythm* of colour.

The colour-intensity of the film is also present in a painterly preoccupation. In the June 1941 issue of *"American Cinematographer"*, Mamoulian wrote about his use of colour in this work. It was his aim to style the film into scenes that would be remeniscent of Spanish paintings. The early childhood scenes are done in the blacks and earthtones of Murillo; the bull-ring is reminiscent of Goya; a chapel is done El Greco-stye, in steel blue, with an elongated painting of Christ above the altar; and the rich vamp's living quarters have the cool, airy space and lushness of courtly life that one sees in the works of Velasquez. This kind of painterly awareness and detail reflects Mamoulian's desire to recreate images whose emotive powers have already been proven; and thereby he reinforces their intensity through a kind of "double exaggeration."

Colour is only one *element* in the visual make-up of a film that can be exaggerated to the Platonic Ideal. Two complete film *styles*, which, when exaggerated to the extreme, become surreal, are the look of "clutter" and the look of "sparsity." The systemisation of confusion (as mentioned by Dali) can be seen in the concept of clutter, and von Sternberg's busy, florid frames bear testament to this. A good example of sparsity is Hitchcock's *The Birds*, where every image contains a minimal amount of elements and is captured with a crystal-clear vision. This vision makes the viewer immediately encounter the image (a shock effect) rather than permit him to gradually absorb it through the clutter of elaborate frills. Along with the idea of the irrational, the Platonic Ideals of clutter and sparsity are the major concerns of the remainder of this book. Before starting the more detailed studies, a generalised exploration of the concepts of clutter and sparsity, along with a look at certain painterly elements in film, and the "limitations" of surrealism, will help in clarifying the surrealist sensibility.

Clutter and sparsity represent two poles of seeing reality. The former exemplifies life; the busy frames of a cluttered work of art are as alive with vibrations as a tropical rain-forest, where vegetation grows entangled and the atmosphere is alive with the hum of a million insects. The latter approach illustrates, if not death, at least a more pessimistic viewpoint; a sparse work of art has the stillness and serenity of a desert landscape where mirages may be glimpsed. In painting, "Venus, Cupid, Folly and Time," by the Italian mannerist Bronzino, represents the ultimate in cluttered vision. Venus is at the centre of the work, and around her are clustered the other three figures, each performing some piece of action (Time unfurls some blue material; Folly is about to toss a bouquet of flowers, Cupid erotically embraces Venus). Every hand in the frame is depicted in an ultra-gesticulating pose; and in the recesses of the painting other images can be seen: a serenely beautiful woman's face floats in a void; theatrical masks; a tortured man shrieks in anguish; two doves; the bottom half of a lion's body. All are fragments of visions, crammed into one frame and draped in flowing material. It is a frenzied vision of action. In film, Buñuel and von Sternberg are the masters of surreal clutter. Remember *The Blue Angel's* stage, with its flying prop-clouds and fat ladies. The stage is so densely packed, so intense with sexual innuendo, that we can almost smell the sweat. In Dietrich's top hat and tails cabaret number in *Morocco*, we can almost feel the intense heat of the place, conveyed in the background by the masses of women lethargically fluttering their fans throughout the number. The China of *The Shanghai Express* is depicted as a land so congested with hordes of people and animals that

"Venus, Cupid, Folly and Time," by Bronzino (reproduced by courtesy of the Trustees, The National Gallery, London)

movement becomes almost impossible.

In Buñuel's films one remembers the riotously disordered (systemised confusion?) bedrooms in *Un chien andalou* (dead carcasses on top of two grand pianos being hauled across a little room by the protagonist, with two frantic *padres* along for the ride) and *L age d'or*; and the living room littered with the fetishistic party guests in *The Exterminating Angel*. This room is the scene of bonfire-building (to cook some sheep which wander in during the course of the film); cello-hacking (for firewood); nail-clipping; piano-playing etc. One woman even carries in her handbag a pair of chicken legs. Buñuel's interest in the disorder of middle-class existence has been a continuing one, and can still be seen in his recent *The Discreet Charm of the Bourgeoisie*, where the party guests now hold their dinner on a stage (in a dream) for the world to see.

The two films on which Buñuel and Dali collaborated are more representative of Buñuel's sensibility; for they are essentially cluttered visions, and Dali, though he has been called a neo-mannerist for the compositions of his works, remains more a visionary of the sparse, which he captures with his expressive use of light. Dali's paintings are crystal-clear and sharp like those of Vermeer (Dali did his own parody of Vermeer's *"Young Girl Reading"* in 1938) to whom he paid *hommage* in *Un chien andalou*. Vermeer is never cluttered, but incisive, sharp and clear; the lighting in his *"The Lace Maker"* is so close to the brilliant sharpness of both Dali's paintings and Hitchcock's films of the late Fifties and Sixties. *The Birds* is completely permeated with this type of striking light.

A comparison of different approaches to the scene of the Last Supper will further illustrate the idea of clutter versus sparsity. The original painting by Leonardo is a fine example of cluttered art. The figures are bunched together, gesticulating, and the table is covered with much food and other articles. When Buñuel recreates this image in *Viridiana* with a hilarious image of the table in long shot, he shows a similar affinity for a cluttered image, with posturing actors (playing a bunch of degenerates) and a full table; it becomes the busiest shot in the film. Compare these two versions to two sparse visions of the same scene. Dali's *"The Sacrament of the Last Supper"* reflects his Vermeer-like clarity of vision. Although the vision is "futuristic" in its interpretation of Leonardo's Renaissance perspective, this does not discount the bareness of the frame that immediately strikes the eye. The stone table has only three articles on it. *The Greatest Story Ever Told* is one of the most extreme examples of clarity of vision in the cinema. Steven's recreation of the same scene is shocking in its simp-

UN CHIEN ANDALOU. Dali's clarity and precision: Vermeer's "The Lace Maker"

UN CHIEN ANDALOU. "The Book Reader"

"The Last Supper," by Leonardo Da Vinci

"The Last Supper" by Buñel. Catholic Clutter.

"The Sacrament of the Last Supper," by Salvador Dali. (National Gallery of Art, Washington. Chester Dale Collection)

"The Last Supper" by Stevens. Protestant Precision

licity: the disciples sit erect and immobile; the colours are almost entirely subdued to a harsh black-and-white; and the table has only a minimum of articles on it. The Stevens and Dali visions have the cold, almost sterile, look of Protestant religious art; whereas the Leonardo and Buñuel visions have the sumptuous, almost decadent, look of Catholic religious art. (Think of the religious art of Spanish America, whose church altars are so heavily encrusted with baroque carvings of saints that they embody the ultimate confusion of Catholic art.) Where Buñuel and Dali have purposely intended to satirise, Leonardo and Stevens have chosen to demonstrate their faith. Through different looks, the same scene (the same informatory content) can convey such contradictory emotions as reverence and irreverence. In both films there is an unearthly feeling. In the Buñuel, it is conveyed through the absurdity of the situation (drunken deformants behaving like religious disciples); in the Stevens, it is conveyed through the director's clarity of vision.

Moments on-screen when a famous painting is recreated always tend to the surreal, for these moments shatter one's expectations of what these images should look like. If one lives one's life believing the Last Supper actually to have looked like the Leonardo painting, then the shock will be great when one is confronted with another vision, be it the Dali, Buñuel, Stevens, or whatever. This concept is related to the seeing of double images, something Dali writes about as being a paranoiac activity where one object can be representative of a totally different object without the slightest physical change in either object. The film equivalent of this idea is not completely exact, for there *are* changes in the elements of the visions; however, what is meant here is that different emotions can be invoked by "relatively" the same image (as in the Last Supper). The new vision is shown on the screen, yet in the mind of the spectator the earlier, programmed vision simultaneously exists; there occurs in the mind a conflict of visions and an irrational juxtaposition. Buñuel uses this device again in the first shot of *Tristana*. It is a long shot of Toledo, the same view as in the El Greco painting; however, El Greco's Toledo was a stormy midnight blue, and Buñuel's is a melancholy dusty brown—different colours for different emotions.

Another type of painterly element that can be used to surreal effect in film is the landscape. Landscapes are meant to be idealisations of the land, and are expressive of certain emotions. The land is endowed with a character of its own in a good landscape. Whether it is the stormy seascapes of Winslow Homer, the verdant pastorales of Constable's English countryside, or the wind-swept Dutch country of Ruisdael, with its massive clouds, these paintings represent emotive qualities in the land that is pictured. It is, however, when the landscape is in disharmony with some other element in the frame, that the irrational comes into play. As was mentioned earlier, in the paintings of Delvaux two realities (one being a landscape) so sharply different, exist together and spark a realisation of the absurd. In films, some dream sequences illustrate this dual reality, where the landscape exerts as much influence on our attention as the character who is set into it. Buster Keaton's *Sherlock Jr.* contains a funny scene of character-landscape conflict. Keaton falls asleep while operating the projector in the theatre where he works; a dream sequence follows in which Keaton is transposed into each shot of the film. It is merely a series of changing landscapes, and as Keaton dives off a rock into the water before him, the scene changes and he crashes into the earth which has just materialised to his consternation. Von Sternberg's films with Dietrich can be seen to contain strange landscapes which exert their own personalities (the *madness* of Imperial Russia; the *fatalism* of steamy Spain; the intrigue of *mysterious* China) while existing together with Dietrich. She always remains the one sane element in these films, filled with madness, drifting from image to image in much the same manner as Keaton, maintaining and creating her own powers of persuasion.

"Still Life" is yet another painting *genre* that can be employed by the cinema. The French call this type of painting "*Nature Morte*"; and how different each sensibility appears. The English term emphasises the life-giving quality of the image, where a precise arrangement of flowers or the twist of a lemon rind are painted so as to imbue these objects with special life; however, the French, with their more pessimistic outlook, think of these images in terms of stillness and death — "Dead Life." They see death as the moment of quiet when the essence of an object is captured. Regardless of whether one sees a painting of this sort to be representative of life or death, one can see the emphasis this *genre* puts on the validity of the object.

In film, both Buñuel and Hitchcock express a similar interest in the intensity of the object as seen in still life. Perhaps Buñuel's interest is more in life and Hitchcock's more in death, but there is some overlap. The Last Supper from *Viridiana* is a good example of lively still life in

SHERLOCK JR. "Character in a landscape." Keaton before he is transposed into the film-dream.

Buñuel; in *Le mort en ce jardin* a picture postcard of the Champs Elysées, held in the hand of one of the fugitives in the jungle, springs to life before our eyes (in a backwards freeze frame); in *L'age d'or* after a *bourgeois* dignitary has shot himself, we see his frozen image plastered against the ceiling. Hitchcock has dealt in still life throughout his career. One thinks of the precisely-composed shots of the man hanging over the edge of the Statue of Liberty in *Saboteur*; and the slight tracking shot into the clasped bronze hands on the dresser in Norman's mother's room in *Psycho*, which acts as a horrific punctuation on the viewer. Both examples show inanimate objects which have been given lives of their own; and when still things spring to life on the screen, or living things freeze solid, the irrational is not far away.

Though surrealism encompasses many aspects of film, some limitations on the *strength* of its influence appear to exist. Compare von Sternberg's *The Scarlet Empress* to Eisenstein's *Ivan the Terrible*. Though both films are set in a bizarre fantasy Russia of the tsars, both are cluttered with baroque images, and both use music for grand operatic effect, the Eisenstein film lacks the irrational juxtaposition of the von Sternberg work, manifested in the conflict between Dietrich (as the sane and pure goddess) and the world around her (filled with mad "heathens"). Nikolay Cherkasov, as Ivan, is *as* obsessed as the world around him. He is well adapted to that world, and unlike Dietrich, does not stand above it. (At the end of *The Scarlet Empress* one thinks of Dietrich in her white riding outfit sitting triumphantly astride her white horse, and holding a banner that flies in the wind.) When we feel with Ivan as protagonist, we feel *part of* the film; and when we feel with Dietrich as protagonist, we feel *outside* and *beyond* the film. *The Scarlet Empress* thus takes us further into the subconscious than does *Ivan the Terrible*.

The external quality of the Eisenstein film, as opposed to the internal quality of the von Sternberg film, is illustrated by two scenes of religious pageantry. The wedding scene of *The Scarlet Empress* takes us into another world, with the droning music of Rubenstein's "*Kamenoi Ostrow*" accompanying the continually-swaying incense-holder that bobs in front of a delicately-laced close-up of Dietrich, a candle's flame flickering by her cheek. We are lulled into a state of hypnosis. In *Ivan the Terrible* a ceremony in a Russian Orthodox cathedral, where Ivan humbles himself before the head priest, is seen much less subjectively. The camera stays mostly in long shot (unlike the von Sternberg wedding scene, which is built mainly of close-ups), and the huge church is filled with hundreds of extras. The scene delights more in the spectacle of the event than in the internal emotions involved, and this preference is representative of the difference between the sensibilities of surrealism and expressionism. The former is an aesthetic that affects the emotions through the mind, and so is more internalized; evocative moods are sought. The latter is an aesthetic that affects the emotions in a less circuitous manner, and so is more externalised; emotions being openly displayed (as we remember the quote from the Eisner book).

Perhaps *Ivan the Terrible* is just too obviously stylised to take us beyond ourselves. It is so *apparently* strange. For example, the incredible opening scene of Part Two, at the Polish Court. Men stand around conferring, and in long shot they are seen as chessmen, placed on a black-and-white chequered floor. They are symbolic figures who have

L'AGE D'OR

been "placed" where they stand, and we are made very much aware of this. The detailing of court figures in *The Scarlet Empress* is much less obvious, though the characters dealt with are no less insane. Remember the stingy priest, the effeminate hairdresser, and the stud-like guardsmen, who lurk in the recesses of the screen or pass back and forth across it without conveying the demonstratively symbolic attitude of the Eisenstein pawns. Eisenstein's heavy stylisation leaves less room for the spectator's mind to ramble; and where von Sternberg conveys the menace of the court through the quick glance of a venomous character, Eisenstein actually paints huge, staring eyes on the walls of Ivan's palace.

Surrealist scenes can be contained *within* expressionist films. James Whale's *The Bride of Frankenstein* starts with a scene that is a satirical description of high "superficiality". Mary and Percy Shelley and Lord Byron sit in a parlour discussing the ending of Mary's *Frankenstein* tale. These chilly characters, so perfectly coiffed and dressed in white satin, sit posed, like icicles of giddy emotion. The high-key lighting enhances the surface gloss of this scene, as do the camera movements, which glide around the great hall while a maid floats, borne by two

IVAN THE TERRIBLE. Grand-scale madness

THE SCARLET EMPRESS. Madness *plus intime*; and a cast of crazy characters

Borzois, along the polished marble floor. As they talk, Mary unravels the end of her story, and the film continues; but the style changes to the low-key lighting effects of expressionism, which persist throughout the remainder of the film. Emotions now become *openly* displayed. The blind fiddler who shows the monster goodness, imbues his scene with such emotional truth that a crucifix in his cottage lights up and glows with a "sympathetic vibration"; and the forest where the monster is chased and caught, is composed of stark, branchless trees, symbolically representing the emotional isolation of Frankenstein. The film continues to be openly expressionist, and only once, toward the end, does surrealism again raise its head: in the double image of Elsa Lanchester, who, having finished her role as Mary Shelley, pops up as the Bride, herself. The fragile and subtle internalisation of surrealism make it take a second place to the stronger expressionist dimension of the film which overwhelms it.

If surrealism's intensity is weakened when mixed with expressionism, it is actually strengthened when combined with naturalism; an exploration of Hitchcock's *Spellbound* reveals this. Hitchcock obtained Dali to create a surreal dream sequence for his film about psychoanalysis. Dali's images for this scene were like those in his paintings: full of sinuous lines: eye imagery; long shadows and a feeling for heightened perspective; and observed with great clarity. Although Hitchcock's vision is generally compatible with Dali's as far as a feeling for shadows, heightened perspective, and clarity is concerned, the final result of this dream sequence was more expressive of Dali than Hitchcock. It is more a painter's dream than a film-maker's, and it is too *obviously* surreal to succeed completely in film. Dali merely recreated the surrealism of his canvas; in film however, a more *concealed* method is needed to express a surrealist sensibility, due to the inherent realism of the film medium—the devices of painted surrealism on film become blatant under the reality-conscious gaze of the cinema.

When a surrealist sensibility is coupled with a more naturalistic look, as in the second dream sequence in the film (this time entirely created by Hitchcock), a more emotionally-involving and nightmarish sequence is produced. In this dream Gregory Peck remembers how he was responsible for the death of his younger brother when he was a child. We see the banister he and his brother sit on. Here we have the heightened perspective similar to Dali, but without the obviousness (jagged gate-posts loom up forebodingly in the foreground; the banister traces a sharp diagonal perspective to the background, where high arches add a further feeling of surreal depth). The next frame, with the

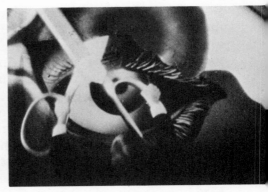

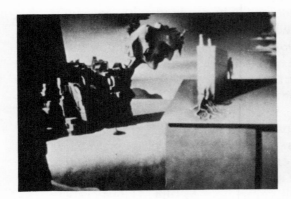

SPELLBOUND. Dali's vision

boy's "huge" feet in close-up in the foreground and his brother quite tiny in the distance, also gives a fine feeling of exaggerated perspective, while the lighting lends a long-shadow effect. One can see how a better concealment of the devices of surrealism is more appropriate to the cinema, where reality is inherently more present.

 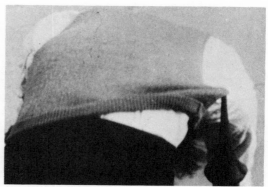

SPELLBOUND. Hitchcock's vision

In Francois Truffaut's interview book with Hitchcock, the latter makes some illuminating statements that concern these scenes. "The real reason [that he hired Dali] was that I wanted to convey the dream with great visual sharpness and clarity, sharper than the film itself. I wanted Dali because of the architectural sharpness of his work. Chirico has the same quality, you know, the long shadows, the infinity of distance, and the converging lines of perspective. . . My idea was to shoot the Dali dream scene in the open air so that the whole thing, photographed in real sunshine, would be terribly sharp." (In the final shooting, it had to be done in the studio.) Years later, in *Vertigo*, Hitchcock was to perfectly capture the feeling of Chirico that he mentions here.

Perhaps all that the Dali dream sequence needed was that it be shot, as planned, in real sunlight, and it would have attained as intense a surreality in its own way as the Hitchcock scene. One will never know; yet this makes one see how even the single factor of lighting can effect the intensity of the "other world" which is sought after and created. Chirico, himself, was confronted with much the same problem as Hitchcock. After spending years studying the master painters of the fourteenth and fifteenth centuries in the museums of Europe, he came to the conclusion that painting in tempera, as they had done, was far superior to painting in oils, as Chirico's contemporaries were doing. He saw how tempera was a better capturer of colour, light and luster, and he lamented the French Impressionists, who thought they could capture all the mysteries of light with their technique, when in fact, the very paint they were using harboured the shadows they wished so much to avoid.

Both Hitchcock and Chirico realise the importance of lighting in conveying their respective surreal visions; that even a slight alteration in this element could reduce the surreality of a work, is a sign of the subtleness of this sensibility.

2

Luis Buñuel

"Once Upon a Time
Eight Years Later
Towards Three in the Morning
Sixteen Years Before
In the Spring"

—Sequence of titles from *Un chien andalou*

Although the vision of Buñuel is influenced by his dense and cluttered style, it is mainly his irrational sensibility, as manifested in his treatment of image, montage and sound, that gives his films their surreal quality. The images in Buñuel's works that are the most intense are evocative of either humour or mystery; and those images that are the most mysterious are also the most beautiful. Buñuel has said that "mystery is the essential element" of any art, and the mysterious quality of many of his images (how they unexpectedly arise from nothing) accounts for much of the beauty of his work. Remember the bare-backed woman sitting in the park in *Un chien andalou*. Is she a woman, or is she a statue? She is so still; and before we can grasp her perfect beauty she vanishes from our eyes, leaving us slightly frustrated, having come so close to perfection, only to have lost it. This question-raising regarding the mysterious is a common feature in Buñuel's films. Often we are prompted by the images to ask, "Who is this man?" and "What is the reason for this?" It is the logician in all of us that Buñuel is challenging. In the same film, after the shocking opening where the eyeball is slit, the title "Eight Years Later" appears, followed by a shot of a young man bicycling through the streets of Paris. We are shown him as though we were expected to be familiar already with this man. Could he be the victim of that mad slicer? His eyes seem fine. Could he be the torturer himself? Buñuel will explain: but gradually, so we are enticed into the mystery of the film.

A similar feeling of mystery and enquiry occurs in *L'âge d'or*, after the audience has adjusted to the opening sequence with the bandits (Max Ernst is the leader of the motley crew) and the pontificating

UN CHIEN ANDALOU

clergy. Buñuel cuts to an extreme long shot of a harbour with a fleet of boats arriving. It is almost a fairy tale image, so delicately do these tiny vessels float. But who are the people in the boats? *They* most certainly appear to know who they are and where they are going, but the viewer does not as yet. The scene eventually unfolds itself (they have come to lay the cornerstone of Imperial Rome). This device of presenting unexplained but enticing images, used so often by Buñuel, is one of the most enigmatic techniques of the cinema. The hermaphrodite who pokes a severed hand in the gutter in *Un chien andalou* embodies mystery most concisely: man or woman? The most irrational moment of mystery in this film occurs when Buñuel cuts from the shot of the protagonist lying beneath the woman who is sitting in the park, to the extreme long shot of a group of men in fedoras strolling through (one man carries a cane and pokes the ground aimlessly with it). It is pure coincidence. One of the great mysteries of the cinema will always remain the question of who these men were and from where they came. They seem to be there with such purpose (even if it is just for an afternoon stroll), but men with such purpose have no right to be wandering through surreal landscapes at such a time!

The irrational is also the source of the humourous images that

abound in Buñuel's work. Flaunting conventional symbols to the point
of blatancy is one form of audacious humour. In this way, Buñuel
satirically revels in his images and becomes one with them. To the
delight of some and the chagrin of others, Buñuel often demonstrates
his obsession with foot-fetishists. In *The Young One* a lustfully-
degenerate Zachary Scott gives the naive girl his smelly socks to wash;
and the first shot of *Viridiana* is a tilt-up along a young girl's skipping
rope, starting from her feet, and emphasising the fetish of the man who
is spying on her. In the same film, Buñuel flaunts the phallic image of a
cow's udder as Viridiana unsuccessfully attempts to milk the cow. Her
hands are afraid of the protrusions; she tinkles them slightly, then her
hands recoil in fear. In this manner, symbols so obviously symbolic
(feet and udder) and intensely sensual (udder) are confronted in plain
view, with no attempt made to obscure them. Perhaps the most blatant
flaunting of a conventional symbol occurs in Un *chien andalou*. The
bicyclist sports a diagonally-striped box which hangs on a cord about
his neck. When the woman opens the box she finds a similar
diagonally-striped envelope inside; and when she opens the envelope
she finds a diagonally-striped tie. Any interest the spectator has in the
mysteries this box contains, prompted by its striking graphic design, is

Magritte-like men stumble across the hero's body

sustained through two further amplifications of this same visual *motif*. Buñuel has lead the viewer along and manipulated his inquisition; but because its obviousness is so apparent to the viewer, he can join in the joke. A similar thing occurs later in *The Young One*, when Zachary Scott takes a tie, luridly flaunted by him for the phallic symbol that it is, from a diagonally-striped box.

If flaunting symbols seems a little trivial or silly, a more pointed anarchistic spirit is displayed in Buñuel's treatment of the establish-   · ment. In *Un chien andalou*, two priests are hauled across a bedroom as they cling to carcass-ridden pianos. As they pass diagonally up and out

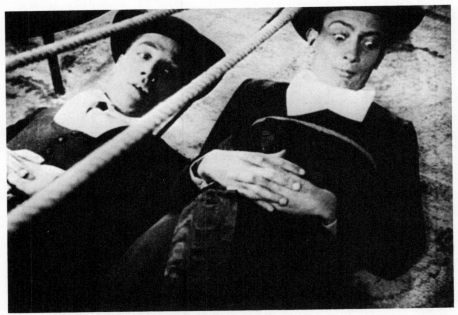

Their smugness cannot help them now

of the frame, Buñuel dismisses religion along with art, in its most conventional form (two grand pianos). In *L'âge d'or* Modot dispenses with a priest by tossing him thoughtlessly through a window. The funniest purely anarchistic image comes at the end of this same film, when the last of the satiated orgiasts emerges from the castle. He pauses on the drawbridge and looks into the heavens savouring the memory of his debauch (and looking for divine approval?). His startl-ing resemblance to Christ, at first unexpected, underlines the hypoc-risy of religion, as the camera lingers with perfect comic timing.

Buñuel's anti-religious stance is his most prominent mark of anarch-ism; but the gash to the human eye shows us, from the start, that *nothing* is sacred.

Imagine the man in the bowler hat

Images irrationally juxtaposed, or conflicting realities, also account for much of the humour in his films. In *L'âge d'or* we see a park, where there stands a stone statue of a robed philosopher balancing a long, flat stone on top of its head. (Recall the stoneware images in certain Magritte works.) A man in a bowler hat walks through the park past the statue, similarly bearing a loaf-shaped stone on his hat. Each man is oblivious of the other, each is in his own world, yet one walks and the other is frozen still. Who is the true creator of this act? Who is the imposter? (Does man create art, or imitate it?)

In *Un chien andalou*, the woman arranges all the articles of the man's clothing on her bed, so as to form an outline of his body. Perhaps he will materialise before her very eyes (stranger things have happened). This simple, plump woman, has appeared to have mastered the power of concentration. The reverse-angle shot of her staring intently at the bed is proof of this; and the man materialises. Another absurdist image in this film is the first shot of the ant-in-the-hand scene: a two-shot of the couple looking incredulously into the man's hand. So intent are they in their gaze that we are lead to wonder along with them. Quickly enough we are shown what they are looking at (ants are crawling from a hole in the man's hand), but at first sight the image evokes a mysterious humour.

The mystery of the hand will soon be revealed

The reserve of the grotesque is another well from which humourous images are drawn in this film. When the hermaphrodite pokes the severed hand, is it not enough that the hand looks so shockingly real? Must it also be covered in a sticky mush at the wrist? (What fun Buñuel must have had between takes, playing with this surrealist prop.)

The logic of dreams is basically the equivalent of the method of montage used by Buñuel in his films. One type of montage relies on the relationships between different visual forms. In *Un chien andalou* Buñuel dissolves between the following images: a close—up of the man's hand, with ants crawling from the hole in it; a woman's armpit; a prickly sea urchin; and an overhead iris shot of the hermaphrodite in the street. All these images contain a central circular element, though the first two are concave forms, and the second pair are convex. This is dream imagery and logic at its most precise and irrational; the flow of images is based only on formal structures. More formal montages occur in the cross-cutting between the sliver-like clouds that pass in front of the moon, and the knife that passes in front of the eye; and in the equation between breasts and buttocks, as the protagonist caresses the woman's breasts which metamorphose into her buttocks under his incessant pressure. Visual similarities alone are enough cause for surrealist effect.

By overlapping locations Buñuel also achieves an irrational mon-

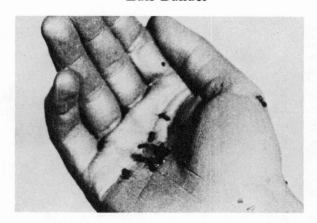

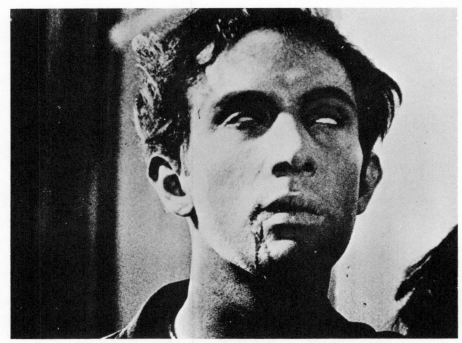

The fall occurs inside...

...and outside

tage. The protagonist in *Un chien andalou*, after shooting his *alter ego*, falls to the floor of the bedroom, seen in close-up. Buñuel effortlessly cuts to an overlap of the falling motion, now occurring in a mysterious park setting. The two locations have been fused into one experience (a similar device was used by Maya Deren in her *A Study in Choreography*), and the emotional intensity of his moment of collapse is heightened. Another example from the same film occurs after the jocular exchange between the couple concerning his mouth and her hair. After sticking her tongue out and waving him farewell, the woman opens the door and a gust of wind whips her hair. Where does it come from? The next shot is from outside the door as she exits on a beach. Through slight disorientation this overlapping location heightens the emotional experience of the moment, and a breath of fresh air is let into a room that was rapidly turning rancid.

L'âge d'or has none of this overlapping montage. In this film Buñuel cuts from one location and time period to another with swift abandon. No sooner is the bandit sequence over than he switches to the arrival of the boats. With a cut we are in Rome, flying over the city in panoramic helicopter shots; and after Modot finishes tearing apart his room, we immediately find ourselves looking at a raunchy, fake castle. The intensity of emotion the film lacks by not having overlapping locations is compensated for by the jarring quality of such shock cuts.

We tend to forget about the sounds and music in Buñuel's films, being so caught up in his visuals; however, his sense of sound is acute (today, with his increasing deafness, he may, like Beethoven in his late years, have an even keener sense of sound). It is not surprising to learn that Buñuel originally came to Paris to study music, since he uses it for ironic effect in many of his films. Both *Viridiana* and *Simon of the Desert* end with scenes set to Fifties beep-bop juke box music, in marked contrast to the austere nature of the rest of the films. Wagner's "Liebestod" is used liberally: the death of the hermaphrodite culminates at the climax of the music (in the soundtrack Buñuel recreated for the film in the Sixties); and as mentioned, the love scene in *L'âge d'or* does the same. In the latter scene, when Modot's face bursts into blood, and ecstasy and frustration are brought so close together, one wonders if Buñuel is revelling in blatant romanticism, and nurturing, besides attacking, his own romantic fantasies.

However, the most surreal use of sound for Buñuel is usually not musical. In *Viridiana* the prayer meeting in the fields (with Silvia Pinal leading the gathering of degenerates and cripples) is cross-cut with images and sounds of construction and destruction, as a new building is being erected on nearby property. Buñuel cuts back and forth between the "worshippers" with their droning babble, and the sounds and images of cement slopping into a dish, mortar being slapped on brick walls, and a sledge-hammer pounding a crumpling wall. This sound montage is of a most exaggerated intensity and has the scattered confusion of a dream. The most satisfying of all his sound effects, however, occurs in *L'âge d'or*. After first seeing a group of archbishops clustered on a rock by the sea, Buñuel goes in close and pans across this grouping. They are mumbling some prayers. As the camera pans this image, the soundtrack is filled with their hypnotic and barely distinguishable babble. The moment is not only humourous, but dazzling and horrendous in its depiction of insanity.

Though an awareness of the irrational is most important for an understanding of Buñuel's sensibility, a knowledge of his cluttered frames adds a further dimension. In *L'âge d'or* the mumbling priests huddled on the rocks, and Modot amidst the flying feathers that he scatters from his pillow, are the most dense images. In *The Young One* Buñuel treats us to a shot where a cute little racoon attacks and kills a hen amidst a clutchy. The racoon then ravenously eats its victim in front of the oblivious flock. It is one shot, stuffed with the heavy intensity of

Inane mumbling has turned these priests into mere skeletons

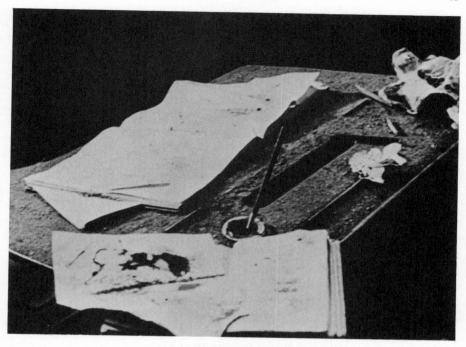

UN CHIEN ANDALOU

feathered animals, and it is held for what seems like an eternity. The intense emotional effect is one of claustrophobia and disgust.

Un chien andalou has its own cluttered room; yet the most cluttered image in the film is one that takes us back through time *within* the room. It is the close-up of the desk that the man sees in the flashback to his youth. The desk represents his boyhood, and he must have been an obsessive, for it is filthy and disarranged. Note-papers are crumpled; pens lie about sloppily; and ink is smudged all over the paper. It is one of the most finely-observed images in the film, and in its evocation of the past neuroses of this man, and in its density, it becomes one of the most surreal moments in the film; taking us into this man's past world (and maybe our own); but just for a fleeting moment; and then it is gone.

L'âge d'or opens with a lurid, cryptic passage, where two scorpions fight to the death, accompanied by ominous music. The titles have a scientific tone ("The scorpion belongs to the class of arachnids. . .") and convey information concerning the quality of this animal's poisonous venom; the fact that it likes to seek shelter under rocks; and that it is basically an anti-social creature. Along with these titles, the use of iris shots to isolate these scorpions endows this mysteriously creepy sequence with a clinical feeling. It contains all the cold precision of a dissecting session, and relates its information in the manner of an illustrated encyclopaedia. (This material *is* actual scientific footage, completely unretouched and unedited by Buñuel)

After this opening, Buñuel drops this objective tone in favour of the more dream-like aspects of his technique; and the spectator is taken away on a subjective-imagistic trip. The objective side of Buñuel is not be forgotten, and this microscopic view represents his continuing desire to make the audience see the truth. This sequence illustrates his split personality: he is at once the subjective surrealist who revels in the intensity of his images, and the objective instructor who seeks to enlighten the world. Critical evaluation of his earliest work generally overlooks Buñuel the documentarian; yet a better illustration of the life of the scorpion could hardly be imagined. Likewise, interpretation of his "documentary" master-piece. *Los olvidados*, generally overlooks the film's surreal nature.

After twenty years of creative problems, and hassling with American studios, Buñuel emerged at the 1951 Cannes Film Festival as the angry iconoclast with his film of slum life and juvenile delinquency in Mexico City, which was seen to be a masterpiece of neo-realism and a powerful social commentary. It was awarded both the director's prize and the international critics' award, as the liberal consciousness of the critics must have been touched. They thought Buñuel had finally emerged from the commercial rut in which they previously saw him — no longer selling himself out, and finally making a socially-relevant statement. How short-sighted these trend-conscious critics were. Did they not know from seeing the glorious imagery of all those preceding films that Buñuel never once compromised his surrealist sensibility? The dreamer of *Un chien andalou* and *L'âge d'or* is also the creator of the stark "realism" of *Los olvidados*. One has only to look to see it.

Buñel as surrealist is not just a man who creates unusual dream sequences that exist within "straight" films. All of his works are infused with this dream-like quality, for it is an inherent part of the man, and could not help but be there for the perceptive spectator to see. The dream scenes are just the passages where this quality is most intense and noticeable. *Los olvidados* is not a semi-documentary with two surreal sequences, but Buñuel's purest expression of surrealism, for it represents better than any of his other films the dichotomy that exists in him, between the objective documentarian and the subjective dreamer, between the anarchistic cynic who destroys old systems and the creative humanist who seeks to build a better world. Throughout this film, these two sides of Buñuel are present, and set off a series of dissonant emotions in the spectator.

The title of the film, literally translated, is not *The Young and the Damned*, as in the sensational title of the English language version, but "The Overlooked" or "The Forgotten." Right from the start Buñuel attacks his viewer's complacency; he is always the unrelenting moralist. The credits contain the statement "All characters in the film are based on real people," and a list of official supervisors from state boards of education and welfare who were consulted during the making of the film. As the credits fade away, however, and the glowing, precise photography of Gabriel Figueroa comes to light, the aware spectator may question the nature of this *affectation* of realism. This is not a documentary though it claims it may be *like* one. It is pure fiction, if one listens carefully, as the brazen theatricality of the opening credit music (so reminiscent in its melodramatic heaviness of the score for *King Kong*) fades from the screen. Official advisors may have helped by contributing their knowledge, but they were not in control of the film-making.

After the tumultuous music has died away, we are immediately struck by the carefully lit set-ups of Figueroa. The images in this film are lit with all the attention to detail and precision that he is known for: shafts of sunlight coming through windows; and deep, dark shadows in recessed areas of the frames. Any comment as to the neo-realist qualities of this film disappear if we consider the visual surface of the film. No De Sica nor Rossellini ever had such a lush veneer on his films of poverty, corruption and deprivation. The setting is the slums of Mexico City, and the location shooting adds a more realistic grittiness to the *milieu*.

The actors appear. Jaibo, the thoroughly corrupt elder youth, is first seen striding down the street, with greasy hair and snakish presence—an early version of the Zachary Scott character in *The Young One*. A thoroughly rotten apple, he shoves his fingers into his pocket, and as they come through the hole in the bottom, they make a sharp, scissor-like cutting gesture (Buñuel will never give up flaunting symbols). As Jaibo is joined by his younger friends and they talk, we become aware of the intense musicality of the Spanish dialogue. It is

Can you hear the music?

recited in a sing-songish fashion that persists throughout the film, enfusing the picture with a dream-like aural quality. The boys may be urchins of the streets, but they are artists all the same, as they bring poetry to the recitation of their language.

The delinquent band attacks a blind man in the street. We are shocked by this graphic depiction of cruelty, but humour creeps in when we realise the blind man to be Buñuel's ever-present representative of convention. The blind man, by nature, sees nothing. He is the pompous Slum Pope, strutting around with staff in hand, lecturing on what is virtuous, suggesting useless magical cures for diseases, and bringing children into submission by tweaking their ears. He is so ridiculous that the attack, violent though it is, appears justified. He cries, ''Have pity for a poor blind man,'' but it is a vacuous sentiment and goes unnoticed. After the beating absurdist images start to appear. In the background rises the steel structure of a new skyscraper; Buñuel once stated that he wished to have a full symphony orchestra playing on top of a building in this film, but the producers disapproved. Although the orchestra is not present, if one is aware of Buñuel's intention one cannot shut the crazy image from one's mind. Is it Nero fiddling while Rome burns? The social castigation implied by this "invisible" image is very powerful, yet the absurdist humour also persists. That Buñuel even considered such an audacious image is a sign of how his surrealist sensibility pervades the entire film.

The camera rests on the fallen victim. He gropes along the ground and looks up at something. The camera tracks back slightly to reveal a hen standing nearby in the street. Man and hen are caught for a moment in each other's gaze, and the scene fades. Seen through the man's eyes, what is this animal *doing* here?! The scene ends with a "dead end" effect: two realities confronting each other with so much concentrated energy; but there is an impasse, a communication gap.

This scene is followed by a further absurdist image, as the thirsty boys take a drink from the breast of a mule. One boy is seen repeatedly suckling as the scene fades. The textual rationalisation may be that the cause of this boy's delinquency is that he needs more motherly love, but we are really more aware of the sensual nature of this image, and how Buñuel revels in it.

Schizophrenia exists within the film in two interesting ways. First, it is a film of dual personality, where there are two protagonists representing different sides of the same personality: Jaibo, the snakish and corrupt "villain," and Pedro, the younger innocent. When Pedro walks through the streets of the slum, with new trust implanted within him by the master of the reformatory, Jaibo suddenly slurks into frame from a doorway, accompanied by ominous music. With the appear-

LOS OLVIDADOS

ance of this *alter ego*, terror is incited in the heart of the spectator, who senses his second self involuntarily taking over.

The second way in which schizophrenia is present in the film occurs in the treatment of Pedro's dream, perhaps the most emotionally-involving dream sequence ever filmed because of its dual nature. It is not the totally subjective dream one usually finds, where the viewer equals the camera and is subject to a barrage of dream images (as in Freder's hallucinations in *Metropolis*, where darting eyes leap from the screen) — but a dream that combines subjectively-perceived imagery with objective reality. Buñuel puts the spectator outside the dream, so that it not only happens *to* (Pedro) the spectator, but the spectator is also *aware* that it is happening to himself. Shot in extreme and hypnotic slow-motion, it starts with a long shot of the bedroom where the dream unfolds; Pedro's bed is in the foreground, and his mother's in the background. From the sleeping body of the boy arises his second self, which sits erect, staring straight ahead, and with a look of incredulous astonishment as the vision materialises before his eyes: the mother arises from sleep and comes to her son. As she stands on her bed, she bounces rhythmically to the springs' movements. As the action is elongated (due to the slow-motion) the impression is given of one gesture actually coalescing with another. She floats off the bed to the floor, rustling her flowing white nightgown and swaying her full, sensuous body as she approaches; she has become a dancer. Pedro says, "Why didn't you give me my MEAT last night?" Buñuel cuts to a shot of the back of the mother as she turns around, with a demoniacal expression on her face, carrying a dripping hulk of flesh. As she glides toward the boy, the room is caught amidst a cataclismic thunderstorm, where lightning illuminates the darkness and wind blows through the curtains and nightgown of the woman, creating a tormented vision. Jaibo appears, grabbing the flesh from the mother, who then returns to her bed. Because the viewer simultaneously sees the dream as a story unfolding before his eyes, and *sees himself* (Pedro) having that vision, the irrational intensity of emotion is increased. We not only experience a terrifying nightmare, but we watch ourselves having it.

The use of slow-motion in this scene is, for Buñuel, an indulgence he rarely partakes in. A long-time believer in naturalism, he avoids "trick" effects in his films, hoping to capture surreal feelings through less obvious devices, such as the intensity of his images, irrational juxtaposition, and use of sound.

After the dream scene, a diversion into a highly-charged surreal state, Buñuel makes a "pretence" of returning to the harsh reality of

The mother as Virgin

slum life, but still persists in infusing the film with his surrealist sensibility. A young girl, sister of the naive child in the *Young One*, rubs milk over her thighs on the advice of the ridiculous blind man who says it is good for the complexion. In the background of a slum street, a modern super-highway is seen. Simple ironic contrast; but in the work of Buñuel can one really separate irony on its informatory level from his totally ironic vision of life?

Buñuel angrily depicts a world filled with the deaf, dumb and blind; not only the pompous blind man, but Pedro's mother. She swats a troublesome chicken in front of her son, saying, "Damn that rooster." This act of aggression to an animal that Pedro loves only intensifies his hate for her. In a blacksmith shop, two boys have a conversation in front of a window where knives and scissors are prominently displayed. It is a world of aggressive and hostile symbols in which they live. One scene in which menacing hostility is conveyed with a disorienting quality occurs when one of the youths goes into the city at night. As he stares into a window display, seen from inside the store, an older man approaches him. They talk hesitantly, though it appears as a mime to the viewer, since the only sound in the scene is that of a violin singing eerily in the background. Suddenly the boy darts across

LOS OLVIDADOS

the street, as a policeman enters the picture and the older man walks away dejectedly. No mention of this scene (attempted pick-up?) is made again, but its mysterious memory lingers.

Pedro's mother is deaf to her son's needs. She tells an authority in her defence, "I work to support my child," but she gets no sympathy from Buñuel, if one remembers his thoughts as echoed by Fernando Rey in *Tristana*, when he states that work is a degrading occupation. In jail, Pedro tells his mother, "Don't be an angel," and again Buñuel shows the world as full of blind symbols. His harshest criticism of the blindness of the establishment comes when he has the blind man curse, "They should be killed before they are born." The pomposity of this silly figure has now become pure villainy.

Buñuel is never averse to leaving the severity of his vision for "comic relief." In one scene Pedro recreates the act of murder by sucking the yolk from an egg and spitting it on the ground. Then, for some unexplained reason, he throws the remainder of the egg right on the camera lens, and laughs distantly. The spectator views the setting through the dripping blurriness of "egg on its face." Does Buñuel really take *anything* that seriously? He may be the cinema's most virulent cynic, but he is also its quietly-laughing philosopher.

"Splat"

While the adult world is oblivious, youth is tortured and dispensed with. On a carousel, children are shown manually pushing the vehicle around for the enjoyment of others. While youths toil, a woman in black formal evening dress *poses* in the background of the carousel. She is the fashion model, and could not care less. A tiny child sits on a cross-eyed horse, laughing merrily. The laughter will stop in a few years when this child comes more under the corrupting influence of the adult world. When Jaibo makes love to Pedro's mother (it is the *alter ego* of Pedro fulfilling his Oedipal desires as manifested in the dream) she stands by her stove, teasingly fanning the heat with her apron.

The insanity surrounding youth continues. We see two dogs dancing in the street, dressed in frilly costumes. Is this not strange? They are part of a travelling street musician's act, but their emphasised presence at this point helps to underline the corruption of the world in which our heroes live. When Pedro's mother signs over her child to the school, she says she cannot write her name. The man says, "Make a cross" (as if that could absolve her of anything). While Jaibo and Pedro have a brutal fight (complete with eye-poking), the blind man pontificates as usual, this time sitting in a dense room crammed with fat women slapping around tortillas; his droning voice is accompanied by the

flip-flop sounds these women are making.

Buñuel paints a world that is obviously disoriented. When Jaibo escapes and is chased by the police, a shot of the latter running past a building is filmed on a slight tilt, so that the structure appears to be leaning over. A few shots later, when Jaibo, alone, passes the same building, the camera angle has been readjusted, so it now stands erect, implying that youth left on its own would go straight.

Jaibo is killed. As he dies, the image of a flowing river passes over him. A woman's voice responds to his "I am alone" with "As always, my son." This is a starkly simple moment and far transcends the reality of the miserable existence of Mexico City slum life, to exist on a more cosmic level, where suppression of all that is true and pure by convention is seen as an inevitable tragedy. A mangy dog appears in the streets, and it is Jaibo's identification symbol: the prowling loner. Buñuel freezes on Jaibo's face. As the despairing music continues, Pedro's mother is seen in the streets of the slum, for her kind of life continues. A cart is wheeled to the top of a rubbish heap and Jaibo's corpse is dumped. The camera pans across a darkening horizon, cut by stark tree branches. The image freezes and the film ends.

If this is a bleak and pessimistic vision, Buñuel's split personality also endows the ending with cathartic release, by his complete and humanistic redemption of Jaibo.

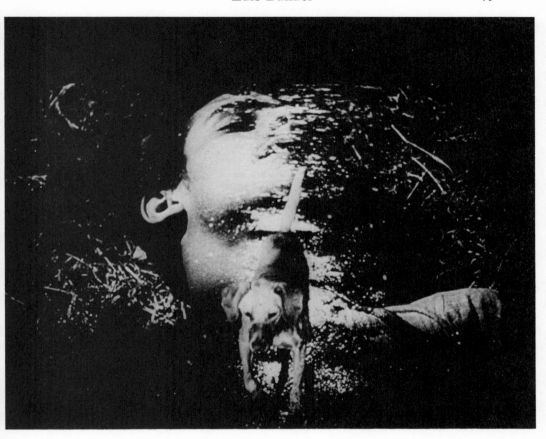

3
Josef von Sternberg

Josef von Sternberg
"I look at the screen, I don't believe I see what I
am seeing, but there it is! I think I am losing my
mind, it is so incredible."
—G.W. Pabst (referring to *The Scarlet Empress*)

Critical appreciation of the work of Josef von Sternberg has been in
continual flux. In the Thirties, his most prolific and representative
decade, when he worked with Marlene Dietrich through a series of
seven romantic films, he was seen by the critics of the period as a
creator of fluff, and as a man who pandered to the romantic and exotic
fantasies of the mass audience. If one looks at the box office receipts
for the von Sternberg-Dietrich films, one can see how they were not
that popular with the public; not nearly so much as the Busby Berkeley
musicals, with their more down-to-earth romanticism. The Berkeley
musical comedies concerned things the Depression viewer could more
easily grasp: characters whose lives were rooted in the hussle of the
city (secretaries, promoters, showgirls), and plenty of wise-crack
humour. The von Sternberg fantasies, however, concerned far-away
lands, with characters and landscapes so unreal to the Depression
audience that they found them emotionally inaccessible. They loved
Dietrich; she was heavenly; but there were no songs they could leave
the theatre singing. (The musical numbers in a von Sternberg film
lacked the singability of the Warren and Dubin scores of the Berkeley
musicals, and the only other music in his films was classical. He used
Beethoven Rimsky-Korsakov and Tchaikovsky, but it was left to
Disney to popularise classical music in *Fantasia*.)

Von Sternberg *was* reflecting fantasies, but not, as the critics
thought, those of the public. He was reflecting his own idiosyncratic
desires, and for those critics who *did* pick up this fact the validity of his
art was questioned, due to its personal indulgence in a time of
economic turmoil, when solidarity was seen to be so important. Von
Sternberg's revelling in pure fantasy was interpreted as if it were some

kind of immoral act. This attitude is very representative of the film
criticism of the Depression, so caught in the conventions of the time
that it now reads like some of the stuffiest and most dogmatic ever
written. John Grierson, though his style was fun and lively, saw von
Sternberg as a great director who became a cameraman; and for
Grierson, the von Sternberg-Dietrich films were merely a string of
beautiful photographs.

In the Sixties Susan Sontag brought out her incredible and unique
"Notes on Camp". In a serious and devotional style she attempted to
define a new sensibility which she saw becoming more prominent in
contemporary man's perception and to give validity to this "unseri-
ous" way of perceiving life and art. Camp was the ultimate example of
making everything theatre, of making everything outrageous. She saw
no division between the sublime and the ridiculous, and put the von
Sternberg-Dietrich films in the category of "art." As time passed,
however, camp took on a derogatory connotation, and liking something because it was camp was seen to be a degrading attitude.
Sontag's good intentions have been undeservedly forgotten. If one
looks at Fragonard's "*The Swing,*" one can see behind it the same
sensibility at work as the one which created *The Scarlet Empress*. In
this film a similar scene occurs (Dietrich, before being sent to Russia, is

"The Swing," by Fragonard (detail). Laughing ladies and (opposite) swinging ladies, in their own florid paradises

seen frolicking in her parents' garden and laughing as she plays on a swing): both visions depict an abundantly-crinolined laughing lady, swinging obliviously amidst lush surroundings. In the painting, one man pulls the swing with a cord while another lies in the shrubbery, awaiting his moment of bliss; a cherubic statue stands in the background. In the film version, giggling maidens dance around the garden. Both visions are not only decadent, but have a level of absurd humour. To deny the validity of von Sternberg would be like discounting the entire output of Fragonard, Boucher, and other painters of rosy-cheeked women. Laughter in appreciation of this kind of art is neither degrading nor condescending if it recognises the basic absurdity of the artist's vision. There is, however, more to von Sternberg than the superficial decadence of a Fragonard; and what Sontag unseriously perceives as the ridiculous, Herman Weinberg seriously sees as the sublime.

In the light of this changing attitude toward von Sternberg's films, we can see how he can be such a difficult director to appreciate, so unique and quirky is his vision. His sensibility combines the sublime and the ridiculous, and as such, is an ironic vision. People who like their comedy "straight" (like the wise-crack humour of the Thirties) find von Sternberg too serious; and those who like their drama "straight" (*The Grapes of Wrath* is a good, morally- uplifting example) find von Sternberg too silly and self-indulgent.

Von Sternberg never saw things "straight." His vision had always been one that was distorted by the passions of love. In *The Scarlet Empress* this is apparent in two striking scenes. The wedding ceremony, where the screen is packed with Russian Orthodox priests carrying religious banners, is one example. In long shot, the image of the crowded church looks as though it were shot with a Cinemascope lens (though none existed at that time) and projected without an anamorphic adaptor, giving the figures an elongated, cramped look. It is an image of verticle compression, accomplished through attention to the verticle elements in the frame. Earlier in the film, Dietrich lounges in her canopied bed, gazing at a diamond necklace she dangles from her hand. The shot is seen through the veils of the bed, and the camera, through selective focus, diffracts a stunning close-up of this woman, through the holes of the lace, into a vision of abstract patterns of light and dark made of the planes of her face. Von Sternberg lingers on this shimmering image, but never long enough for the insatiable viewer.

Von Sternberg is an acquired taste, like wine. The more exposure one has to his personal vision, the more one can find to relate in his films. Irony, ever-present, is the most subtle of emotions, and ac-

THE SCARLET EMPRESS

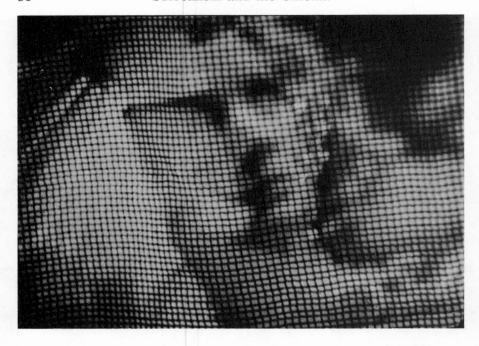

counts for that quality which makes von Sternberg's films hard to grasp. Irony pulls the emotions in different directions. Sado-masochism is a continual theme in von Sternberg's work; from the tortured Professor Rat in *The Blue Angel*, who makes a rooster out of himself by crowing on stage for the woman he loves (who in turn tortures him with her infidelity), to Don Pasqual in *The Devil Is a Woman*, who, after warning a young lothario of the dangers of his former seductress, Concha Perez (Dietrich), returns to her himself, again to be subjected to her fickle whims. Throughout this film dolls and puppets are shown to be representative of this sado-masochistic tendency. (The screenplay is from a novel by Pierre Louys called *"Woman and Puppet."* It is interesting to note that this same author provides the source for another erotic film, Gregory Markopoulos's *Psyche*, a film of homosexual love.) The doll is the ultimately manipulated "person." In *The Scarlet Empress*, in the early part of the film, when Dietrich is still under the control of her parents and protectors, she acts with marionette-like gestures, tossing her head back and forth in response to others. In this fetishistic interest in dolls von Sternberg resembles the surrealist artist Hans Bellmer, who makes constructions from reassembled pieces of mannequins, dolls, bits of lace, hair, roses, etc.

The ironic concept of fallen nobility is another facet of the sado-masochistic attitude of von Sternberg. He realised the world no longer held a place for nobility (the professor dies; Pasqual, the military man, is made a fool), yet in the living of his own life von Sternberg exerted such style as if to counteract that. (This probably arose from his own feelings of insecurity, and it was common knowledge in Hollywood that von Sternberg was one of the least secure men in that city of the insecure.) Photos of him on the set of *I, Claudius* show him wearing high leather boots and a Hindu turban; and who will ever know the truth behind the ''von'' in his name? He saw himself as the forgotten patrician of aesthetics. In his relationship with Dietrich this ironic vision of himself must have found its ultimate illustration. He had created her (so he thought); she was his doll; however, through public response and the workings of fate, *she* went on to become the living legend, who would become the beacon that would throw new light on *his* films for new generations of filmgoers.

Von Sternberg's ironic vision is even present in the look of his films. Although the visual surface of his films is lush, he is not an extravagant director. Never was there such a master at making so much of so little; and it is ironic that this hedonist should also be such an economist. (How different from Erich von Stroheim, who would spend thousands of dollars to achieve the slightest effect.) In *The Scarlet Empress* von Sternberg economically created crowd scenes of rioting Russians by incorporating footage from Ernst Lubitsch's *The Patriot*. Although his use of lace fog, smoke, tree branches and fish-netting is representative of his desire to clutter, it is also representative of his economy of effort. Studio moguls must have loved him, for he gave them films of splendour for relatively little money. It was in his use of light, however, that von Sternberg created his lushest patterns; and light is the cheapest and most accessible commodity on any film set.

A detailed study of *The Devil Is a Woman* will reveal von Sternberg's mastery of cluttered vision. In his book on the director, Herman Weinberg quotes the Uruguayan film critic, Emil Rodriguiz Monegal, on this film: ''This is the masterpiece of Josef von Sternberg, directed with the greatest freedom. It offers in all its glory the absurd Spain of the foreigner—Spanish music *à la* Rimsky-Korsakov in the background, the German Marlene as an improbable Andalusian en-

THE DEVIL IS A WOMAN. Dietrich shimmers

chantress, and Goya and Spanish baroque as seen through the eyes of a German Expressionist.'' The film exists on may levels as a surrealist film experience, much more than just being the absurd vision of a foreigner, although this is one element of its absurdity. The constant change of costumes is another level of absurdity in this film. From one Travis Banton creation (the same designer of Spanish costumes for Mamoulian's *Blood and Sand*) to another, Dietrich is in a state of perpetual metamorphosis in this film. In no two scenes does she appear the same; always in black, white, or black and white; but the look, with changing hairstyles and make-up; is always different. Concha, like a moth, flutters from one setting to another, ephemeral and hard to grasp.

The Devil Is a Woman is an extension of the "Liebestod" scene in *L'âge d'or* — a full feature on the agony and ecstasy of love and honour, set amidst the Spanish landscape of severe fatalism, with mad-house qualities. It is one of the most romantic films ever made, and self-indulgently so. Von Sternberg revels with masochistic melancholy in the suffering of his male lead Don Pasqual (played by Lionel Atwill, who even looks like the director, with 'his short-cropped beard). Pasqual is constantly loved and left, taunted, tormented and teased by Dietrich's Concha throughout the course of the film, and only at the end, in his sick bed, does Pasqual realise the perfection and integrity of this woman.

The setting is not really Spain, but von Sternberg-Spain, and as such it becomes the visual metaphor for a mad-house, with the cramped and stuffy feeling of a dream landscape of claustrophobia. For a film that is not a spectacle, it is packed with many extras. The opening carnival scene starts with an image-laden pan from streamers and little dolls suspended in mid-air by parachutes made of balloons, to a riotous crowd of merrymakers, some of whom wear huge, grotesque masks. Confetti is strewn everywhere, and in one area of the fairground some police officers are roped together as a group of Bruegellian pranksters dance a ring around them. From this opening alone we can see this is no run-of-the-mill festivity, but an insane last fling at life. When Antonio (Cesar Romero) first enters, the congestion of the scene is enhanced by a forceful tracking shot of him trying to make his way through the crowd. Because he is pure vanity his strides carry him through this maze; but a maze of bodies it still remains.

The congestion never ceases throughout the film. The over-crowded tobacco factory is one example. Is von Sternberg over-crowding for socially conscious reasons? Being the visual hedonist that he is, one finds that unlikely. Remember the train interior, where a static Diet-

Cluttering interiors...

rich sits with sublime integrity (under a meticulously-placed baby spotlight) amidst a seething mass of life: the dancing gypsy, who crosses the screen with her exotic movements; and the general feeling of the masses behind her, shuffling and breathing heavily. It is a breath that is truly *felt*; the atmosphere reeks of humanity. Throughout the film stairways are crowded and filled with movement, and von Sternberg is constantly panning along them (like the one in Concha's hotel, alive with guests).

Besides packing his images with people, von Sternberg jams the frames with other elements. The carnival at one point seems on the verge of being engulfed by the confetti that is draped everywhere. When Dietrich makes her first entrance in a carriage filled with balloons, there barely seems to be enough room for her in the seat. The cafe where she sings has a steamy marine *motif*, seen in the erotic nude mast-heads and steering wheels that clutter the place (direct from *The Blue Angel*).

Much of von Sternberg's clutter is used to obscure the spectator's vision, and in this way he provides us with his version of Buñuellian mystery. At one point Concha teases Pasqual by dancing flirtatiously before him, swishing her lace *mantilla* continually in front of the camera lens; and at the start of the torrential rain storm (during which Pasqual eventually beats up and "rapes" Concha), a scene similar in atmosphere to much of von Sternberg's own *Docks of New York,* Concha's stairway is seen through a maze of craggy vines.

The Platonic Ideal of clutter is still most perfectly embodied in that shot of the snowbound train. Snow almost engulfs the train, and telegraph poles sink dismally into the drifts, as a man struggles through the landscape. A close contender for the most dense image in the film occurs at the end of the carnival scene. A dream-like dissolve leads from a shot of a caterpillar-float which hangs above a crowd of noisy merrymakers, all festooned in confetti, to a totally silent "after the ball" shot of the same area. Down a long, wide stairway runs Concha,

...with pelicans thrown in for good measure

draped in the mystery of this isolated, yet slightly swaying landscape (as wind gently rustles the streamers).

To match the visuals in their rich decoration, von Sternberg creates a soundtrack which is ear-popping by any standard. It is not only cluttered, but exaggerated to a point of insane intensity. He takes his music from Rimsky-Korsakov's "Caprice Espagnole", and its some-times fatalistic, sometimes capricious moods make the perfect com-plement to the visuals. The opening credits use the main theme from this score: at the start the sound is full and richly-orchestrated, but by the end of the credits has been gradually thinned to a solo piano, playing the final trills with the lightness of a scherzo. Music is again used well in the train scene, where the gypsy dances enticingly in front of Concha (another lesbian undercurrent, like the woman kissing a top-hatted Dietrich in *Morocco*?). Spanish guitar music, dulcet voices mumbling in the background, humming and foot-stamping all help to create the heaviness and intense claustrophobia of this scene.

Perhaps von Sternberg's greatest coup in the use of sound is his imaginative use of simple room tone (background sound), to comple-ment the masses of people who cram the frames, in a hubbub of mumblings to match. The carnival is a riot of indistinguishable scream-ing noises; the casino (where the three characters finally confront each other upstairs in Concha's room) has a background noise of inane chatter. All this vague chattering has the same disorienting effect as the mumbling archbishops in *L'âge d'or*. It is vaguely disquietening, and jars the consciousness; we cannot grasp the meaning of this chatter, yet it pervades our senses during the entire course of the film, and becomes as maddening for the spectator as it must be for the characters within the film. The ultimate in bizarre mumblings comes in the to-bacco factory, where the crowded women workers are heard creating a mass of chit-chat; but if one looks closely one notices that not a girl is actually moving her lips! Knowing von Sternberg's perfectionism, it seems unlikely that this was merely an oversight in re-dubbing, but a purposeful use of heightened sound, irrationally juxtaposed over non-talking images. This use of sound has as much of the mad-house quality to it as the cluttered visuals.

Not only are voices used as room tone, but other sounds as well. The bar, where Antonio and Pasqual have their private conversations, has an atmosphere of pure silence, the heavy and deadened quality of a sound-proof booth (or more appropriately, a padded cell); the intensity of this silence heightens the sounds which occur in the following scenes (the flashbacks, which are filled with blaring noise). This aural contrast between hushed silence and deafening noise, gives the film a unique *rhythm* of sound.

Von Sternberg not only exaggerates the sounds and silences, but extends them in time. After Concha's song in the cafe, the audience applauds thunderously for a period of time that may be thirty seconds (and seems like an eternity). At the end of the "rape" scene, the camera is placed outside the closed, rain-soaked shutters; we can hear the rain, and over this the sounds of Pasqual beating a sobbing Concha. Here, too, the sounds are extended for an unusually long period of time, ending the scene on a disturbingly sick note.

Sound used for punctuation is still another way in which von Sternberg creates an aurally intense experience. During the carnival scene, Concha flirts with Antonio from a distance, as she pops the balloons in the carriage in which she sits. There is much cross-cutting between the two, underlining the innuendo of the scene. All the while the soundtrack has been filled with the inane babbling of the surrounding merrymakers. We wonder what Dietrich's first line will be. The droning continues, until she finally tosses her head back and laughs enticingly. A laugh at this point in the soundtrack becomes an intense punctuation to the preceding scene, and embodies all the mystery of this woman in one sound (similar in effect to Jane Wyatt's laugh on the balcony of Shangri-La, as Ronald Colman first enters, in Capra's *Lost Horizon*).

Shrill, razzing noises on the (horns) are also used to punctuate the action. During the confrontation scene in Concha's room above the casino, Pasqual is masochistically scorned on the soundtrack by a razzing horn in the casino below, and again, at the film's end, as the train leaves with Antonio alone, spurned by Concha, the engineer's horn blows mockingly over a close-up of Antonio's hurt face

The thunder and rain of the "rape" scene give tremendous intensity to the violence of that scene, and at one point Concha shouts out the word "love" to Pasqual, but a thunder clap obliterates the word. Finally, voices themselves are used as punctuation. Concha's one-eyed boss at the cafe heightens for Pasqual the insanity of his situation. As he tries to buy Concha back from this woman he asks, "Concha — how much?", only to have the woman respond with an incessant, hen-like cackle. The scrivener, to whom Concha dictates a letter meant for Pasqual, droningly repeats every single phrase to her in a dulled monotone. This repetition is totally unnecessary on any level, save the emotional effect, which is truly bizarre. This is the sound equivalent of seeing double images; we hear the same words, but uttered with completely different voices and inflections.

Von Sternberg has always shown a flair for the irrational. Remember the last shot in *Morocco*, with Dietrich flinging her past to the wind, as she leaves her high-heeled slippers behind in the desert sands, to walk off in pursuit of Gary Cooper. This fragile beauty could never really brave the hardships of a desert sandstorm so unequipped but somehow, the removal of her awkward shoes makes the whole thing plausible, in an absurd way.

The Devil Is a Woman is not to be outdone in its depiction of an irrational landscape where lovers grapple with the torment of passion. The use of masks throughout the film lends an irrational touch; especially in the balloon-breaking scene between Concha and Antonio. His mask is black and hers is white; and the constant cross-cutting between the two faces, and the subtle exchange of taunting and vain facial gestures, lend an absurd feeling to the game they are playing. Even extras wear masks (in the carnival scene a man in a rooster suit chases a woman). The most irrational use of a mask occurs when Concha is delivered a letter by a woman wearing a grotesque pig face. The woman stands by the door for a while, her head bobbing up and down aimlessly, and then leaves without so much as saying a word. In the background can be heard the jumbled voices of the revellers. We are astounded by this absurd image. Who is this woman in the pig mask? She is treated so matter-of-factly by von Sternberg that her obviously odd presence is even further heightened. If she is no one special, then she is just another extra; and if she is just another extra, then she must be representative of everyone else downstairs. If so, then the entire world must have gone mad.

Irrational images which dwell upon futility help to emphasise the fatalism of the story. Not only are the major characters caught in fateful webs (of confetti?), but even the most minor extra seems to be doomed. During the great snowbound shot, an anonymous little man struggles across the field of snow, a study in uselessness if ever one existed. The most futile moment in the film occurs in the first scene at Concha's "mother's" house. The scene starts with a shot of a man carrying baskets of live chickens up the rickety steps. We have no idea who this man is, or what he is doing (he is delivering the groceries, it is soon revealed); we simply see the Platonic Ideal of frustration, as this poor little man struggles under his burden of cackling, flapping hens. The image is cluttered beyond belief, and though he finally reaches the top, it is hardly a victory.

Irrational montage is not used too often in this film, but its most prominent occurrence provides a jarring effect. It occurs at the end of the confrontation scene in Concha's room. The strange woman in the pig mask has just left. As the scene ends (a duel has been arranged between the two men) a razz is heard. Von Sternberg cuts to a shot of a

Game-playing: card tricks and masks

small group of masked men, lounging by a wall, looking casually about, with the same kind of aimlessness to their glance as that of the pig woman. He then cuts to a long shot of more merrymakers in masks. Had the order of these last two shots been reversed, the effect would not have been as disorienting (for the long shot would then serve as an establishing one); however, the cut on the razzing noise to the specific shot of this odd and mysterious group of men (again treated so nonchalantly as to heighten their importance) has a disorienting quality. Who *are* these people? We have been conditioned by the rest of the film to the merrymaking atmosphere and the mask *motif*; however, to have this image of strange disorientation follow so closely in the wake of the pig woman, would seem to confirm our worst fear—that she *was*, in fact, truly representative of "the others" in the film, and everyone else *must* be insane by now (these men being the proof).

Although von Sternberg may revel in his romantic fatalism, he also knows when to laugh at his own absurdity, flaunting his symbols with the same vitality as Buñuel. The masochistic puppet *motif* is used practically to the point of flagellation. A hand from nowhere pops from a window to deliver to Antonio a message in a jack-in-the-box; and Pasqual playfully fiddles with a hand puppet in one of his confessional monologues. The metaphor of Pasqual as a bull (he brutishly kicks down Concha's door in the "rape" scene) is flaunted in the slightly low-angle shot of him standing in the doorway to her room above the casino. Behind him, on the wall, hangs a bullfight painting.

Verbal puns and witticisms occur occasionally. Pasqual refers to Concha and her "mother" at one point as "there they were, bag and baggage"; and in Concha's room, before Pasqual bursts in, Antonio tells her, "You're not going to play cards with me, are you?" It is so slimy and conniving a remark, and so filled with innuendo, that Buñuel may have consciously borrowed it to close his own *Viridiana* ("I knew someday that my cousin Viridiana and I would play cards together."). The levity of these jokes, their very silliness, is a sign that von Sternberg, as fatalistic and morose as he may become, never forgets the absurdity of his existence. He is still the creator of films that express the passions and joys of life.

4
Alfred Hitchcock

"We all go a little mad sometimes. Haven't you?"
——Norman Bates in *Psycho*

The later films of Alfred Hitchcock (especially *Vertigo* and *The Birds*) show a very *American* vision. Whereas Buñuel's sensibility is effected by Spanich fatalism and a Marxian-Freudian influence, and von Sternberg's sensibility is mostly an insular, escapist one, Hitchcock's attitude is one based on paranoia; and although this is probably the result of a strict Jesuit upbringing, one feels that given the generally threatening nature of the American way of life, Hitchcock's move to the United States in 1939 furthered and solidified this paranoiac vision.

In America Hitchcock found not only his maturation as an artist, but also an environment that was visually better suited to his needs than the English surroundings had been. The English films show Hitchcock to be slightly at odds with his artistic environment, and reflective of nothing of British art trends of the time. In the late Twenties and throughout the Thirties the British art scene was fairly inconsequential, being dominated by pseudo-futurists and pseudo-cubists, neither trend being at all compatible with Hitchcock's interests. It is not inappropriate that it was in Germany that he directed his first two films (*The Pleasure Garden* and *The Mountain Eagle*); a country whose expressionistic sensibility better mirrored Hitchcock's own attitudes than his native land. The remainder of his films stand out from the British art scene, and by his use of extreme close-ups and gliding camera movements, Hitchcock started to establish his own unique visual style. The only quality the films of this period reflect (and it is an unfortunate one at that) is the mediocre mechanics of British cinema (the muddy blacks and whites, the unsure special effects).

When we look back on the American period we see a director who, though still very much his own man, is reflective of other artistic influences around him, and is more a part of his environment. In Hitchcock's uncluttered images, depicted with clarity and precision,

"Western Motel," by Edward Hopper (reproduced by courtesy of Yale University Art Gallery)

and in his depth through shadow, we can see certain similarities with the American painters Grant Wood and Edward Hopper. All three artists have bleak visions of America; and their lonely landscapes represent the isolation of the individual in America. The severe woman sitting stiffly on the bed in Hopper's "Western Motel" could as easily be Janet Leigh in the motel room in *Psycho*, so threateningly vapid are the surroundings. In the same film, the mansion on the hill, with its remote and stoic position, is Hitchcock's own interpretation of Wood's "American Gothic." Wood's "Young Corn" shows rolling hills and farmland in cool lime green, under the yellow sunlight and long shadows of an approaching sunset, and could easily be the same northern California landscape through which Tippi Hedren drove in *The Birds*. If England lacked an artistic framework within which Hitchcock could find himself at home, the United States provided him with a surrounding which was more conducive to his bleak vision.

As already mentioned, Hitchcock's sensibility is one based on paranoia and fear of the unknown; and his reaction to the void that appears when all that is known is stripped away, is to fill that gap with images. The images that Hitchcock chooses are limited to those which he sees as the most *essential*; and only the barest minimum of shock

PSYCHO. Waiting; stark and rigid

elements is shown to the spectator, with such a clear and tight view that the emotions evoked (be they fear, shock or disquietude) become too intense for a rational acceptance and must be experienced subconsciously.

Man's fear of the unknown is most archetypically represented in Hitchcock's starkest film, *Psycho*, the ultimate paranoid vision. That shower jokes have become a part of our generation reflects not only the power of Hitchcock's influence, but the truth behind his insights. The translucent shower curtain lets in only so much light; but not enough to reveal the complete truth.

One finds the unknown, mysterious, prompting questions; and the characters in the film search out the answers to their questions behind the mysterious doors of the mother's bedroom and the fruit cellar of this American Gothic house. The black sunglasses of the cop who interrogates Marion Crane on the highway are a visualisation of our fear of what lurks behind hidden things. The most chilling element of the unknown occurs when Lila Crane is searching through Norman's room. She sees the room of an obsessive (Norman Bates is a close kin of Buñuel's protagonist in *Un chien andalou* with his messy school desk) where a large teddy bear is propped on a dishevelled bed. She picks up a record from the player, Beethoven's "Eroica' — and with a subliminally schizophrenic allusion, Hitchcock conveys not only Norman's delusions of grandeur, but also his strange sexual nature. ("Eroica" means "Heroic"; yet so briefly is this word flashed upon the screen that we also feel its resonance as "erotica".) After establishing the mysterious framework of this room, Hitchcock then has Lila pick up a large, black, hardbound book. She studies it. There is no title on the binding. She opens it to the first page, and an expression of extreme anxiety crosses her face. Cut to the next scene. No mention of the book is ever made during the remainder of the film. This cut signifies a terrifying moment, where the progression of revelations about Norman's "sick" character is suddenly and mysteriously stopped. What could this book possibly be? This incompleted passage instills a most insidious disquietude in the spectator, and a lingering fear of the unknown.

Hitchcock balances subjective and objective perception with truly paranoid inconsistency, by altering the spectator's identification in a scene. Think of his use of alternating tracking shots (as Lila approaches the house in *Psycho*; as Melanie Daniels approaches the ranch in *The Birds*). This device gives both the subjective view of approaching an element of the unknown (as it gets nearer the viewer finds himself desiring the object more), and the objective view (where the spectator finds himself confronted with his own blind stupidity and desires a rejection of the object). This kind of device is only one way in which Hitchcock manipulates his audience's emotional response within a scene. He often does the same thing, more subtly, without even cutting. In *Shadow of a Doubt*, Uncle Charlie, whom the audience suspects of being the murderer of rich older women, sits at the dining room table, lecturing his niece Charlie, and her family on the stupidity and uselessness of matrons. It is a long speech, filled with seething resentment. As he talks, the camera tracks in slowly on his profile until the screen is filled with the side of his face. As he ends his speech he turns his head, totally without reason, and delivers the final line full-face to the camera. It is only at this point that the spectator realises that it was to himself that the speech was directed. Without cutting Hitchcock has switched viewpoints from the objective to the subjective with paranoid repercussions. Seen objectively (and in profile) this leering story remains just a story, and is not personally threatening; however, once confronted directly with the reality of its attack, it becomes intensely and internally felt.

Before exploring *Vertigo* and *The Birds*, the following humourous sidetrack should serve as further elaboration on Hitchcock's personality. In Truffaut's interview book with Hitchcock, the latter explains that he has long been a practical joker. On the occasion of his wife's birthday he took six couples to dinner, having hired a woman to dress up as an elderly dowager and take one of the seats at the table. Her job was just to sit there. No one but Hitchcock knew about this woman, and he did not talk to her once during the entire evening. The guests started to wonder who she was, and why Hitchcock was ignoring her, finally realizing it must have been one of his little jokes. In the book, Hitchcock confesses that he has dreamed of a variation on this joke (though he has never had the nerve to do it) where he would not only ignore the woman, but take great malice in scolding her drinking in front of the guests, tell her to go to her room, whereupon she would burst into tears. This absurd sense of humour is also present in his films. In his blackest work, *Psycho*, Norman Bates. the murderer who masquerades as his dead mother, tells Marion Crane, "Mother. . . what is the phrase?. . . isn't quite herself today." In any discussion of Hitchcock and his bleak vision, we must not lose sight of the man as a practical joker.

Hitchcock's sense of humour is most sustained in *North by Northwest*. Cary Grant, as Roger O. Thornhill, finds himself involved, through coincidence, in a world espionage scheme, and his adventures throughout the film take on the characteristics of a paranoid's nightmare, in which he is constantly being chased, attacked and mistaken for a man whom he does not even know. The ultimate in absurdity occurs in the crop-dusting scene, where Grant, standing in the middle of a totally barren prairie, is suddenly made the victim of an attack by a low-flying crop-duster. The absurdities of this film climax with a chase over Mt. Rushmore. Grant and Eva Marie Saint crawl around the earlobes and nostrils of such dignitaries as Lincoln, Washington and Jefferson, and toward the end there occurs a Hitchcockian cliff-hanging scene, which must surely be a visual definition of "the stretch factor"; that is, exaggerating reality beyond normal suspension of disbelief into the surreal world.

Vertigo and *The Birds* not only contain a wealth of surreal elements, but also exist as complete surrealist film experiences. Both are dream films: the former, a deliberately paced and profoundly disturbing dream; the latter, a shocking nightmare.

A brief plot outline of *Vertigo* is first necessary. Scottie Ferguson (James Stewart) has resigned from the San Francisco police department due to acrophobia, and becomes involved in a case for an old friend; his job is to shadow the friend's wife, Madeleine (Kim Novak), whom he is told is a suicidal neurotic who believes she is possessed by the spirit of a dead woman—Carlotta Valdes—whose portrait hangs in

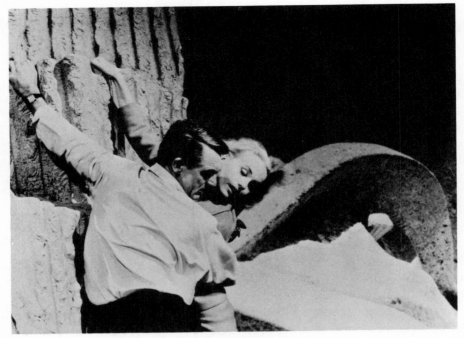

Someone is watching over them

the local art gallery. Scottie falls in love with this woman, but is unable to prevent her death, due to his fear of heights, when she falls from the steeple of a church. Scottie, overwhelmed with guilt, has a nervous breakdown, but is nurtured back to health by his old girl-friend Midge (Barbara Bel Geddes). Soon after, Scottie sees a girl on the street who exactly resembles Madeleine, but who disclaims any knowledge of her. Scottie is attracted to this second girl, Judy (also played by Kim Novak). At this point, the audience learns something that is still kept hidden from Scottie: Judy and Madeleine are actually the same person; Judy, being the mistress of Scottie's friend, was part of a plot to have the friend's wife murdered in a way that would have Scottie believe he saw the *suicide* of this woman. Scottie, not knowing this fact, tries to make Judy in the exact image of Madeleine, whom he still loves. He finally becomes suspicious, and in an attempt to make Judy confess takes her back to the church and forces himself to lead her to the top of the steeple, where she accidentally trips and plunges to her death.

Beneath the superficial outline of a suspense film lies a most profoundly disturbing evocation of dream-world existence. Vertigo (dizziness from heights) implies a simultaneous fear of falling and an attraction to it; and in its dual nature is a correlative with death, which one is both fearful of and attracted to. Scottie is similarly attracted to a woman who at first represents death and then *is* death itself, as he tries to bring her back to life. Madeleine represents for Scottie the fascination of Death Idealised, and his recreation of Judy in the former's image is the illustration of this. Throughout the film Scottie lives in a fantasy world, and through Hitchcock's various methods of identification the spectator is made to partake with Scottie in this dream-world existence.

The irrational nature of some of the plot elements in the film is a sign of the other world with which we are confronted. When Madeleine dies half-way through the film (like Janet Leigh's sudden death in *Psycho*) we are completely surprised, believing Kim Novak to be the major female star in the film. Where do we go from here? As we are experiencing together with Scottie at this point, our question is soon answered in the form of his nightmare and mental breakdown. Again, when the plot twist is revealed to the viewer, and identification with Scottie is severed, the floor drops from under our feet. If Judy was really only impersonating Madeleine, then why does she act so strangely throughout the rest of the film? We realise that Judy was not

In this studio portrait from VERTIGO our hero appears to be in a quandary (Can you blame him?). See the swirl in Madeleine's hair

just acting Madeleine, but *being* her. It may have been another *persona* of herself in which she was subsumed, and this accounts for her odd reactions during the film. (Is her fear of returning to the church a fear of being revealed as the accomplice, or a fear of being totally submerged in the Madeleine *persona*?) All of Judy's actions from this point become ambiguous, and in the remainder of the film reality and illusion are similarly combined and indistinguishable.

Hitchcock's clarity of vision finds an ideal representation in *Vertigo*. If he tried for the Chirico quality in *Spellbound*, he truly reaches and surpasses it here. In the long, wordless sequence (accompanied only by Bernard Herrmann's haunting score) where Scottie follows Madeleine around the city, the surreal landscapes of Chirico are most noticeable, and give the sequence an otherworldliness of its own. Subjective tracking shots take us to quiet and empty locations: an art gallery, a graveyard, a Spanish church, an old house (once belonging to Carlotta Valdes). All these exteriors are shot late in the day, when a low sunlight casts long shadows and a golden glow, giving the scenes their feeling of deep perspective. Every location is empty and hushed, and Madeleine drifts through the landscapes like a dream (which she is, in fact, to Scottie). At the graveyard Hitchcock uses a greenish glow, which he later echoes when Judy first appears as a made-over Madeleine. It is a colour reminiscent of Chirico. The melancholy mood of this sequence also pervades the scene at the Golden Gate Bridge, where Madeleine attempts suicide and is rescued by Scottie.

Later, the pair go to a sequoia forest; again the mood is quiet and still. The towering trees, make a fine counterpoint to the minuteness of human life that walks amongst them. Madeleine's hands pass over a cut cross-section of trunk, illustrating the passage of centuries, as she points to where she was born (similar to a moment in Chris Marker's *La jetée:* "That is where I come from.") She has pinpointed the moment that life represents, as opposed to death, which is so much longer-lasting. The attraction to Scottie (and the spectator) still persists as the scene ends with the couple walking through the golden-lit sequoias, which cast their long, dark shadows all around.

The nightmare scene that Scottie experiences is equally precise in its vision of dream reality. It is animated with a very harsh and sterile look. The most shocking image occurs when the bouquet of flowers (an image held by the woman in the painting, and similarly held by Madeleine when she visits the gallery to study the portrait), colourfully drawn and seen from above, suddenly bursts into abstract pieces and starts to swirl in a dizzying vertigo effect, like something from *Fantasia* gone mad. This effect is used throughout the film and be-

"Mystery and Melancholy of a Street," by Giorgio de Chirico

Madeleine's attempted suicide: lonely figures in a mechanical landscape

comes another precise visual image—not only in the nightmare, but also in the opening credits (the spinning graphic design) and in the hairstyle worn by Carlotta Valdes and Madeleine. It is a bun-like style with a definite swirl. A vertiginous device is also used (with a dizzying effect on the spectator) in the simultaneous track-in zoom-out shot down the centre of the church's stairwell, which is representative of Scottie's own distorted vision.

The final scene of the film with Scottie peering down from the top of the steeple, having conquered his vertigo, is the most chilling. He is precariously perched on the outside of the ledge clawing at the frame for support. Storm clouds are gathering in the background and the wind is whipping his clothes. His face registers pure horror. If Scottie has conquered his literal fear of heights, his nightmare is just starting, for with the realisation of his truths, he has lost his illusions (both Madeleine and Judy) and is now confronted with the void that remains.

If the visual surface of the film looks like a dream, the *mise-en-scène* is even more unreal. Hitchcock uses the device of irrational juxtaposition to maximum effect: memorable are the subjective tilt-pans when Scottie watches Madeleine sitting in the barren art gallery studying the portrait. The first tilt-pan goes from the bouquet on the bench beside

Madeleine to the bouquet held by the woman in the painting. The
second one, even more precise (aided by its vertigo imagery), goes
from the swirl in Madeleine's hair to the very same image in the

painting. Reality and illusion are shockingly juxtaposed; yet, as we later find out, Madeleine's reality is not so "real," for she too is just an illusion (Judy in disguise). Thus, our first conception, is, *in reflection*, shattered.

This type of irrational juxtaposition is used again, for a pathetic-humourous effect, when we see a painting that Midge has done. It is her parody of the Valdes work, with her own pragmatic face used instead of Carlotta's. Her face shows the same kind of startled look as the Alfred E. Newman cover caricature of "Mad " magazine ("What, me worry?"). In one shot we see this silly painting and Midge in the same frame. She has done this to show her lover how absurd his obsession is, but being as seriously involved in this dream by now as he is, the trick only hurts Scottie and alienates him more from Midge. In one swift shot these emotions are conveyed in the contrast between the absurd painting and the real, pragmatic woman. The film climaxes with the epitome of irrational juxtaposition. Judy has now been transformed by Scottie into Madeleine. They are about to leave for dinner, when Judy mistakenly puts on a jewelled necklace worn by Carlotta in the painting, and which was one of Judy's props for the trick she was playing in the earlier part of the film. The view is subjective as Hitchcock cuts from the necklace seen in close-up, as reflected in a vanity mirror, to a match-cut of the necklace in the Valdes painting. The camera then tracks back to reveal the empty art gallery, with Madeleine again sitting immobile, the bouquet at her side, studying the painting. Illusion and reality are here so richly entwined that description becomes difficult. Hitchcock has tied together the past elements and emotions of longing after the dream (Madeleine-Death) and the present reality of Judy. Not only does Scottie see her necklace and *imagine* the one in the painting, but the necklace is seen reflected in a mirror (a further level of illusion). We cut from reality (Judy's prop necklace, which was also part of a big hoax) reflected in a mirror to a painting; then track to see Madeleine studying the painting, knowing now that this is not Madeleine but Judy. This is Scottie's realisation and moment of truth, and although the viewer had this fact revealed to him earlier, this graphic confrontation of the many-leveled reality serves to astound the spectator as intensely as it does the protagonist.

The Birds represents a nightmare of a more obvious nature. Melanie Daniels (Tippi Hedren) is the rich, bored, San Francisco playgirl who tries to snare Mitch Brenner, (Rod Taylor) who lives with his possessive mother on their ranch near Bodega Bay, a small fishing community north of the city. They first meet in a bird pet store, where Melanie pretends she is the salesgirl and tries to sell Mitch some love birds. She follows him to his ranch, and with her arrival masses of birds start appearing and inflict a series of attacks on the village throughout the remainder of the film. In the end, after the deaths of numerous people, Melanie, Mitch, and his mother and sister drive off into the horizon, leaving behind thousands of waiting birds, which seem to have won.

As Hitchcock has stated, the theme of this film is human complacency. The emotional effect on the viewer is one of pure paranoia. We are constantly attacked, not only by the birds (through audience-character identification) but by every single visual image in this most precise film. We leave the picture emotionally beaten-up; empty and stunned. If a question of morality arises here (is it "right" for the film-maker to make his audience sick?), it is left to the individual to decide upon the validity of such a brutal attack. (One feels that those who find the film morally objectionable are probably also the most complacent.)

That the birds come and go with no apparent reason, and attack without immediate warning, is the essense of the irrational plot of the film. Within this structure the characters lead absurdly determined and futile lives; and as the spectator usually identifies with these characters, though Hitchcock through alienation effects steps back occasionally to provide us with a more objective look, our shock at the hopelessness of these people's lives is intensified. Hitchcock shows us these people as puppets. Back projections (and obvious ones at that) are used occasionally (only behind Melanie) to bring her out of the film to underline her complacent qualities, her petty whims and mannequin-like nature. Specifically, in the roadside conversation scene between her and Mitch's old girl-friend, Annie Hayworth, Annie is always seen photographed with her back to her little house, filmed on location; alternating shots of Melanie sitting in her sports car are all studio shots with back projection. Back projection is used again behind Melanie when she is first attacked by a gull while crossing the bay in a motor boat. Her total indifference to the birds, an attitude she displays toward everything else in her world, is underlined by this alienation effect, which not only takes her out of the main body of the film, but makes the audience also step away and look more objectively at this silly girl.

The most noticeable use of an alienation effect occurs when the birds come flying down the chimney of the Brenner home. It is the only scene in the film where the special effects are weak, where we can sense the phoniness of it all. (The actors performed in a barren room and the birds were matted-in later.) Whether intended or not, the unreality of this scene is unmistakeable, as displayed by the gestures of the actors, which must have been thoroughly under the director's control. As they run about this small room, striking out at the air, hitting birds away, their actions (due partly to their acting when the birds were not there, and having to "pretend") are frantic and puppet-like, jerky and confused. We sense the two levels of reality in the room: the actors "faking it" in an empty space, and the birds fluttering about unmolested in a peopleless room. It is a subliminal effect, not without its force, and shows us how separate the two worlds are, and the horror and confusion that occur when these two worlds collide. Later, before the final bird attack, the characters wait, trapped in a boarded-up house. Suddenly, bird noises are heard. The ensuing scene recalls the one mentioned above, and before even one bird can penetrate into the house, Mitch runs about the room, pushing his mother, sister and Melanie into chairs for their own protection. It is done in a wordless pantomime, as they react with fearful and frantic jerkiness. This odd effect recalls the actions of the earlier scene, but without the added dimension of the presence of the birds. They are not needed now. Their shock effect has been sufficiently established to make this scene even more terrifying than the former.

Hitchcock heightens the irrationality of his film with sound devices that are similar to those used by Buñuel and von Sternberg. The droning and repetitive children's ditty "Risselty-Rasselty" that is heard coming from the school as Melanie waits outside by the playground, unaware of the growing flock of crows on the jungle-gym behind her, acts as a hypnotic effect of hopelessness, and heightens the inevitability of the birds' attack on the children. Hitchcock, not being a lazy one in flaunting his symbols, peppers the opening scene of the film, the game-playing between Melanie and Mitch in the pet store, with more different images of birds than any other, and humorously, by overstatement, foreshadows the horrors to come. Not only does the characters' conversation revolve around buying some love birds, but in one shot of Melanie we can see in the background birds in cages; bird paintings hanging on the wall; and birdseed food boxes with brightly-painted budgies on the covers on a shelf. (Birds, birds, everywhere.)

Other absurd touches in the film include one silly moment as Melanie drives her sports car to the ranch, with the two love birds in a cage on the floor next to her. As she rounds a sharp curve, Hitchcock inserts a close-up of the two birds from behind, perched on their little bar, swaying back and forth to the rhythm of the curve (how those little fellows are able to adapt). The beauty of the unexpected is most fully realised in a typically Hitchcockian red herring. Early in the film when Melanie sneaks into Mitch's hotel room in the city to deliver the birds, she rides in the lift accompanied by a suspicious-looking creep with a thin moustache. Looks are exchanged but nothing said. They both alight at the same floor but when he notices that no one answers the door she is knocking at, his harsh glare turns quickly into a most amiable grin, and he explains to her that Mitch has gone to his ranch. He has become such a friendly helper.

The acute vision shown in *Vertigo* is even more apparent in this film. Every shot is so clear (if slightly in soft focus in the close-ups of Melanie to heighten her superficial gloss) that Hitchcock never needs to use selective focus, even in two character conversations. The spectator sees everything that the director wants him to see. Melanie's drive to the country contains long panoramas of eerie landscapes, shot with a low sunlight; the first sight of Bodega Bay has low grey clouds hanging over it. With the passage of time, the landscapes become more surreal. The final shot of the film, when the characters drive off into the horizon through a bird-infested landscape, occurs at dawn. Rays of light stream down to earth from thickly-amassed midnight blue clouds. As far as the eye can see there are birds. A crow cackles; and "the end" appears on the screen.

Mention must be made of the soundtrack, which consists not of music but of bird noises (cackles, shrieks and wing-flappings) all electronically manufactured. This synthetic use of sound, by its exaggeration, transcends realism in effect. For the final shot, a silence is *heard*. Hitchcock used a monotonous low electronic hum that is only vaguely audible; and the effect of pure silence is as unique here as it is in von Sternberg's padded cell sound of silence in *The Devil Is a Woman*. Though Stanley Kubrick brought the moog to the knowledge of the general public in 1971 in *A Clockwork Orange*, his "genius" is only second-hand; in 1963 the quiet genius of Hitchcock was inconspicuously doing the same thing.

The clarity and precision of the images is most effective in those moments of greatest shock effect, for the most horrific are ironically (and invariably) also the most visually beautiful images. The most startling of all occurs when Mitch's mother (Jessica Tandy) finds a man dead in his home, his eyes pecked out by the birds. It is a silent sequence, and as she slowly enters his place, shock images of violence and destruction are intercut with her movements, eventually climaxing on three shock shots of the dead man lying on the floor amidst his blood and the dead birds. It is a cut-away to the broken window in his room that most interests us here. The screen shows a window frame: the pane is shattered, and wedged between some broken glass is a mangled bird with dripping blood. The shot lasts less than one second, but the care with which the prop was prepared is most apparent. This is highly-arranged reality, where every element in the frame has been meticulously placed. The lighting is clear and bright, and the effect is similar to that of those "window boxes" some artists make. The *assemblages* of Joseph Cornell are one example. (Cornell himself made a number of surrealistic-imagistic shorts in his lifetime, some in collaboration with Stan van der Beek.) Cornell created little memory boxes of paraphernalia and frozen time. Two basic features of this type of image are the importance given to the frame, and the quality of stillness. In this shot from *The Birds*, we find Hitchcock as master still-life painter; we could call the shot "Dead Bird in Glass." Not only do we see the image within the screen's frame but also within the frame of the window. When one thinks of double frames one also thinks of Magritte, who has done many paintings (for example "Euclidean Walks") where a frame is put around some scene within the frame of

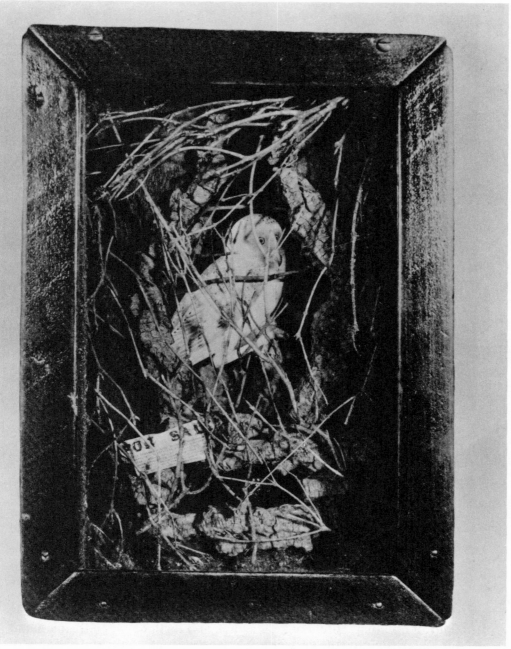

"Untitled (Habitat with Owl)," by Joseph Cornell. A world within a box.
Courtesy Doris Starrels, Los Angeles

THE BIRDS: a frame within a frame enhances a highly-arranged reality
(compare with Cornell picture previous page)

the painting itself. Hitchcock's bird-in-glass image is later recalled
subjectively when Melanie is in the phone booth, and a huge gull comes
flying straight into the glass, shattering it before our horrified eyes.

Every shot in the film has this precision of vision, though the shock
moments, as mentioned, are the most representative. Even Melanie's
make-up has this quality of precise arrangement, remaining unruffled
and unsmudged throughout the film (even after her final attack in the
attic). Although this emphasises her mannequin-like character, it also
visually serves to make every frame she is in more intense in its precise
quality.

Other shock moments of stunningly-observed reality occur when
Melanie and the others in the cafe are looking through the window
(again the framing device) at the petrol station, where a man is unknow-
ingly lighting his cigarette beside a pool of spilt fuel. The suspense is
tight, if obvious. Hitchcock cuts back and forth between the man and
his match (lighting the cigarette; blowing the match out; and eventually
throwing it down) and the silent Melanie behind the window. The two
cut-aways of her are less than half a second in length; they may even be
freeze frames so imperceptible as to be subliminally shocking. The

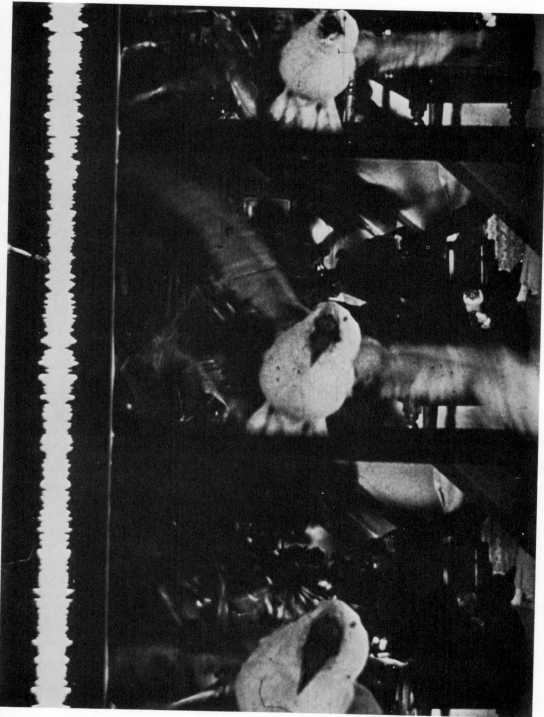

editing is so sharp, and the "freeze" shots of her in close-up, her expression going from fear to intense shock, so grotesquely exaggerated and intensely compressed, that the moment of combustion is too much to take intellectually. The moment is literally stunning.

As if the shock effects of the imagery were not enough to make the spectator feel assaulted, Hitchcock also employs subjective identification devices to aid in this feeling. The alienation effect has already been mentioned with regard to Hitchcock's taking the viewer beyond the film for a more objective look at the horror; but the spectator still spends most of the time in a subjective reality, experiencing the horror. Hitchcock uses his standard parallel tracking shots (as Melanie approaches the ranch; as she ascends the stairs to the attic) but also a less subtle effect that is more shocking by the very directness in which it attacks the audience. These shots come out of the film itself and "speak" to the spectator: the shots of the birds flying directly into the lens (in the phone booth; and in the attic, when a gull comes flying into the lens in close-up, mouth open wide). In the cafe scene, Melanie and some customers confront the man who suggests that they "Kill them!" (the birds). They look at him (the camera) with puzzled expressions and are, in fact, confronting the viewer with the problem of what is to be done. Later, in the same scene, the worried mother goes into a tirade against Melanie about how it was she, the "foreigner", who brought the bird attacks with her from the city. We see this harried housewife shouting frantically into the lens at *us*; accusing *us*. If *The Birds*, with its sledgehammer paranoiac effects and its brutalising exaggeration does not really make us think, it does make us *feel*.

5
Samuel Fuller

"The cinema is like a battleground. Love. . .hate.
. .action. . .violence. . .death. In a word: EMO-
TION."
                                    —Samuel Fuller (in *Pierrot le fou*)

"I know I'm drunk, but my brain's O.K."
                        —Dolores Dorn (in *Underworld U.S.A.*)

The ultimate sparsity of fictional film can be seen in the works of
Samuel Fuller, where such an extreme sparsity exists that it becomes
elemental. Fuller is a primitive artist, who reduces all the elements of
his films to their basic, most crude level. For him there is no gloss
beyond what is necessary; and his films have the simplistic quality of
comic books. To see a film by Fuller is to experience the absurd effect
of a comic book brought to life. As with famous paintings recreated on
the screen, the double image made in one's mind of what a comic book
should look like, and what is actually shown on the screen, is an
irrational juxtaposition which incites an emotional response (be it
laughter, shock or excitation) in the spectator. The look which one has
become used to seeing on a newsprint page now suddenly springs to
life on the screen. Other films which have a tendency toward this
quality are Lang's *Metropolis,* with its childish idealogy and dynamic
compositions; and Vidor's *The Fountainhead*, with its high contrast
blacks and whites and its basic Ayn Rand love-hate relationships.

Fuller handles film technique in much the same way as the French
surrealist painter, Clovis Trouville, handles paint. Both artists appear
to be "bad" at their craft. Trouville paints sacreligious paintings of
lustful nuns smoking cigarettes and displaying garters on their shapely
legs, and grotesque carnivals of hallucinatory images in lurid colours
that reek of madness. His brushwork is somewhat laboured and one is
aware of that; his technique appears to be one that has not been
mastered, though a better description would be that it is a technique
that has *stopped making any pretence* of capturing reality. Fuller's
technique, as sharp and dynamic as it is, is likewise very visible. He

has totally given up trying to render things smoothly realistic (a trend that increases with every new film). In two works he incorporates 16mm home movie footage shot while on his travels. A "dream" scene in *The Naked Kiss* illustrates a romantic story of Venice. From the contemporary American living room where the story is being told, Fuller cuts to his home movie footage of Venice's canals. The change in stock is obvious, for the smooth faking of reality is not what interests Fuller here, but the feeling of the contrasting worlds that this shift in stock generates.

Although Fuller provides us with little nuance or shading, he does provide us with an intense immediate experience which is rooted in his visual style and sensibility. It is an attitude that is base, simplistic and elemental; yet ultimately shocking and forceful. It is a vision based on exaggerating sparsity to a point where it becomes one of the most intense of all film experiences.

One may question this notion and merely attribute this sparsity to the limited budgets of his B-films. Economics does prevent Fuller from making lavish pictures, but it is not a very influential factor in the final look of his work. He *could* clutter his frames more than he does but he choses not to. By studying the elements of his movies we can see this primitive quality of sparsity.

Fuller's themes are universal, and so stripped of complexity that they can be grasped by the simplest mind. *Underworld USA* can be summarised as a *revenge* film. Tolly, played by Cliff Robertson, having witnessed his father's gangland slaying when he was a youth, effects a plan of revenge, with the help of the police, on the killers involved, who have now become leaders in "the mob". All of Tolly's actions are motivated by a one-dimensional drive toward his goal and this limited emotional impetus is responsible for the driving force of the film. *Shark* is a film about *cynicism*, a story of double-crossing in a remote African sea coast town, where a group of no-goods search for buried treasure. The only motives of the characters stem from feelings of cynicism. Even the most peripheral characters are bastards. For example, a peasant woman who appears in one scene and is paid compensation money for the death of her son while he was helping the main characters in their search for gold, slyly counts her cash and suspiciously eyes the woman (Silvia Pinal) who pays her off. No one escapes Fuller's wrath.

Underworld U.S.A. is a one-level revenge film, while *Shark* is a one-level cynicism film. As one critic has stated, Fuller's themes are generally of the gutter, and the emotions he evokes are of the gut. His politics are simplistic and his plot devices are the most contrived; yet all this one-dimensional crudeness is so purely conceived and executed that the whole becomes a totally cohesive vision.

In establishing character traits, Fuller tries for the barest of archetypes. He aims to immediately establish the personalities of his characters in their introductory shots by employing some prop or device to quickly set down their type. (His schooling in newspaper journalism equipped him for the job of keeping things crisp and concise.) Cigars are a common Fuller prop used to establish character. Gela, a mobster in the gangster film, chomps endlessly on a cigar to give him a tough-guy quality — Fuller's only attempt to give him an extra dimenson beyond the dictates of the script — and the little boy thug in *Shark* who becomes the protagonist's (Burt Reynolds) sidekick is first seen in a severe low-angle shot as he smokes a cigar—smoke issuing menacingly from his mouth. Gee, he's tough! This use of the little boy is a device used by Fuller in his earlier *The Steel Helmet*; it is the kind of simple identification device used in comics to give children a means of relating to the adult heroes—for example, Batman and Robin. Again, in the same film, Fatso, the huge proprietor of the cafe, is introduced by one of the most vulgar shots in cinema: the screen is filled with red. The camera zooms out to reveal Fatso lounging on a bed with his harem; the red spot where the zoom started we now realise to be his crotch. With minimal effort Fuller establishes the lewd nature of this man. Even in the naming of his characters Fuller reflects the world of the comic book: Tolly and Cuddles are the lovers in the gangster film, and names used more than once in his films are Griff, Grant, Candy and Skip. With names like these (and personalities to match) it is sometimes shocking to hear Fuller's characters, an assortment of prostitutes, child molesters and thugs, spouting quotations from Goethe and Shakespeare, or appraising the works of Beethoven in their more melancholy moments. When this happens, the characters are reflecting Fuller's own interests outside film. He is not only crudely emotional, but also crudely intellectual.

In his creation of "atmosphere shots" Fuller makes a good contrast with von Sternberg, his exact opposite. This kind of shot, usually a long shot, requires that the director set the *mood* of a scene in a manner similar to the way he establishes the personality of a character. Whereas von Sternberg clutters this type of shot, Fuller is sparse. In *Shark* we find a dusty African café. The set has one spinning fan on the ceiling, two wicker chairs and a table; and Arthur Kennedy as a drunken has-been doctor sporting a red fez. All the essential elements needed in the recreation of a dusty African cafe are here, and no more. This sparsity comes not from cheapness, for many cheap films are

made that lack Fuller's feeling for the elemental. His early career was
also one of low-budget projects, but then he hid his lack of funds better.
In *Shock Corridor* a stripper does her act before a curtain, her only
prop a full-length mirror. Even the cheapest movie could afford the
luxury of another prop (a chair, a couch, a few figures in the foreground
to represent the audience which is so obviously not there), but Fuller
refrains from doing so, for it would interfere with his vision of the
strip-joint as an arid place, lacking any warmth.

   The surface tonalities of these two films further reflect the world of
the comic book. The gangster film is shot in black-and-white (a supreme achievement by Hal Mohr), but there are really only three basic
tones: pure black, pure white and pure grey. The film lacks the variety
of middle-tone greys in most productions; it is so essentially a "black-
and-white" film (like *Psycho*). *Shark*, shot in colour, has only three
prominent colours in it: red, yellow and blue, the three primaries—the
three colours used most in comics, and in the comic-influenced works

The hair of some comic book people has an unusual way of turning grey. "Spider Man." Copyright © 1970, 1974 Marvel Comics Group. All rights reserved

So too in the films of Samuel Fuller

of neo-Dada pop artist Roy Lichtenstein.

Elements of make-up further carry across this feeling of primitive-
ness. Gela's hair has the prematurely grey look that some comic book
people have with a sharp synthetic line of division between the black
and white.Silvia Pinal (a long way from the subtleties of *Viridiana*)
finds herself playing the sublimely crude ideal of the cheap, cynical,
comic book broad: yellow hair (not blonde), pink lipstick, and one
strong line of black eyeliner on each eye-lid. Another interesting use of
make-up is the exaggeration of facial bruises. In *Underworld U.S.A.*,
Pickup on South Street and *Shock Corridor,* Fuller paints black and
glossy bruises on the cheeks of brutalised victims, heightening the
intensity of the pain.

The use of shadows is also basic. The killing of Tolly's father, in the
opening of the gangster film, is depicted in huge, menacing shadows on
the wall of an alleyway. Comic book illustrators also delight in this
form of simple and direct effect.

Though Fuller is not beneath using symbols, he does seem unable to
use them subtly; and it could never be said that he flaunts his symbols

Right: "Iron Man."
Copyright © 1971, 1974
Marvel Comics Group.
All rights reserved.
Below: SHARK: Silvia
Pinal as the doll with the
gun

UNDERWORLD U.S.A.

humorously, like Buñuel, von Sternberg and Hitchcock. He may
flaunt a symbol, but Fuller has no sense of wit about it. In *Shark* Barry
Sullivan conspicuously munches a banana during one conversation
scene. Though he is standing in a market place, the use of this specific
prop does not flow from the action of the scene; it is planted in his hand
(by Fuller) for the simple shock of its literal symbolic value. In the
gangster film, the clenched fist of the protagonist is used repeatedly as
a symbol of revenge; and in the same film an old souse, who acts as
Tolly's surrogate mother, decorates her little room with baby photos
and tiny rubber dolls. This woman, who so obviously never had any
children of her own, would love Bellmer. A slick killer for the mob
dons a pair of dark sunglasses to absolve himslef of guilt before he
performs his dirty work. Even in his use of signs as ironic counterpoint
to action, Fuller is the crude symbolist. In *Underworld U.S.A.*, when
Tolly, as a youth, commits a robbery, he passes a conspicuously-
placed sign that reads "Give Blood Now"; when he dies, shot to death
in the gutter, he knocks over a rubbish bin with the sign "Keep
America Clean" on it.

The love scenes in Fuller's films have the same over-heated quality

UNDERWORLD U.S.A. Brazen shadows

"Captain America." Copyright © 1941, 1966, 1974 Marvel Comics Group.
All rights reserved.

as those of the "True Romance" variety comics. In *Shark* one moonlit
love scene occurs on a beach. The camera pans down across the sea to
the sand, as the surf laps against the lovers in their bathing suits. Violin
music accompanies the scene. Some dialogue follows, and the woman
slaps the man violently, only to immediately lunge at him and passionately kiss him. The love-hate crudities are as comic bookish as they are
in the writings of Ayn Rand. As they embrace, the surf rolls in to cover
them, and though the aware viewer may think of *From Here to Eternity*
(and Billy Wilder's funny parody of the beach scene in *The Seven Year
Itch*), in *Shark* it is played straight. *Underworld U.S.A.* has its own
share of hot sex, with Dolores Dorn, as Cuddles, the archetypal
gorgeous dish, drunkenly sucking icecubes as she flirts with Tolly.

The fight scene is a standard element of comic books and action
films. Fights are the complete opportunity for a director to let loose
and create a power-house of action. In comic books the fights are
usually shown from many and odd angles, with much flying through
the air in an attempt to give extra life to the frames. The fight in *Shock
Corridor* has much of this flying quality, as do the three (!) fights in
Shark. Burt Reynolds is an experienced stunt man and Fuller often
employs his talent in creating fights that are crudely violent and
action-packed. Fuller goes straight to basics by having Reynolds

SHOCK CORRI-
DOR. Leaping . . .

. . . and flying,
"Spider Man."
Copyright © 1972,
1974 Marvel Comics
Group. All rights re-
served.

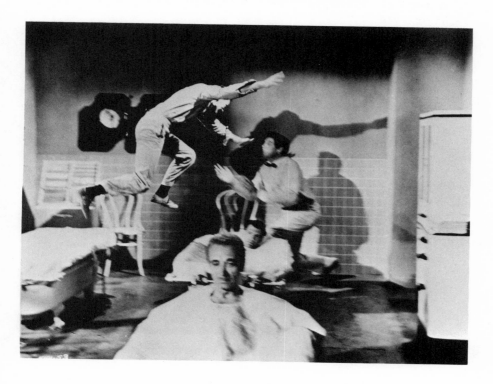

"Vault of Evil." Copyright © 1954, 1973, 1974 Marvel Comics Group. All rights reserved.

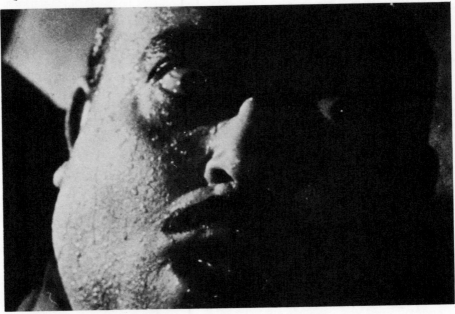

The look of a man about to be incinerated

punch Silvia Pinal out cold at the start of the first fight. As Reynolds continues to battle an attacker, Fuller heightens the spectator's emotional response to this brutal fight through various means: actions are broken down into numerous shots, taken from a variety of odd angles (the frequent cut-backs to the room seen from directly above give the effect of men being trapped like mice in a cage); the cutting occurs on the moments of greatest impact; and regular, slow and fast motion are all used in combination.

The use of dynamic angles in scenes of less power is also used by Fuller to add spice. The extreme low-angle shot that introduces the boy in *Shark* is one example. In the same film one scene shows Arthur Kennedy going through his weekly "DT's," and Fuller obtains a very graphic effect through the alternation of over-head shots of the room (again the mouse-in-the-cage effect) and close-ups of Kennedy running around like a chicken with its head cut off. The use of wide-angle lenses for this scene adds a further dimension of distortion.

Acting styles in Fuller's films run the gamut from very broad to hammy. While Paul Dubov, as Gela, hams his way through the cigar-chomping role in a crude manner, we sense that Cliff Robertson, a more aware actor, had great fun in portraying this exaggerated caricature bent on revenge. The dialogue in both films is extremely intense, without shading or wit.

The use of close-ups is Fuller's most typically comic book device. Comic book illustrators love to bring their viewers in close, expecially to the eyes, that most elemental of all body areas to be portrayed by the penetrating gaze of the close-up lens. In *Underworld U.S.A.*, besides the clenched fist *motif*, there is the eye imagery. We are first introduced to Tolly as a youth in the midst of a theft, by an *extreme* close-up of his anxious eyes. When we first see him as an adult, it is in an overpoweringly intense shot seen from the inside back wall of the safe he is robbing. The door opens, and his two eyes slowly creep over the edge of the shelf. Another fine use of comic book close-up occurs when Gunther, another gangland leader, is killed. He is to be incinerated in his petrol-drenched car. The match is lit and tossed. For a split-second Gunther's terror-striken face is illuminated (it is night) as he goes to his death. The shot is accompanied on the soundtrack by a brief, frantic gasp.

The ultimate in comic book close-up in a Fuller movie occurs in his western *Forty Guns* (see Godard's perceptive review of this film in "Cahiers du Cinéma;" where, by the simple structure of his prose, he captures the comic book quality of a Fuller film). In this work there is

Comic book editing: always the eyes "Nick Fury." Copyright © 1968, 1974 Marvel Comics Group. All rights reserved.

the standard show-down on a western street. Fuller cross-cuts between the advancing party in long shot, and the protagonist, seen in
extreme close-up: his two eyes and the bridge of his nose—a true
composition for the wide screen. This cross-cutting between extreme
close-ups and long shots is a standard comic book editing technique.

Cross-cutting is used in *Underworld U.S.A.* in the scene of the
murder of a little girl on her bicycle, and turns this sequence into a
horrifying emotional experience. The girl is shown riding her bike on
an empty street; then Fuller cuts to the killer's car pursuing her. As she
gathers speed (and the music builds in intensity), so does the car: from
bike tires to car tires, and from girl to killer, the images alternate. The
intensity builds until the pitch is so great that the actual moment of
impact could not possibly be shown, and instead, we hear the noise of
the impact over a shrieking shot of the girl's mother leaning from her
window as she witnesses the crime.

A final element of similarity between Fuller's films and comic books
is the idea of direct confrontation with the spectator. Fuller attacks his
audience in much the same manner as Hitchcock does in *The Birds*,
and attempts to make shots actually "speak" to his viewer. *The Naked
Kiss* opens with a prostitute making-up in front of a mirror (the lens).
When she proceeds to attack her pimp, Fuller uses wild, savage
subjective shots from the man's point-of-view. As an opening to a film
this takes courage. *Shark* also has its share of audience-attack. One
establishing shot of a market place has a peasant carrying a cackling
hen through the street, ending with the bird blotting out the lens.
Underworld U.S.A. has a final shot that zooms to an extreme close-up
of Tolly's dead, clenched fist. It acts on the spectator like a call to
action, and almost punches us out of our seats in the theatre.

Fuller's single-mindedness of vision, as realised by the interaction of
all elements of his film, gives his work the consistency of a master; and
in their depiction of comic book reality, his works help to bridge the
gap between purely fictional cinema and the animated film.

"The Spirit." Copyright © 1974 by Will Eisner

THE NAKED KISS: attacking the spectator

6
Animated Film

"As large as life and twice as natural."
—Lewis Carroll ("Through the Looking Glass and What Alice Found There")

Animated film encompasses as great a variety of styles as non-animated cinema. Though animation usually implies the use of single-frame (stop-frame) photography, this is not a steadfast limitation, and the necessity of a film camera *can* be eliminated by painting directly on the celluloid (as in the films of Len Lye and Norman McLaren); and though animation usually deals in inanimate objects or drawn images, human beings can also be animated through pixillation. McLaren's *Neighbours* is an illustration of the of the pixillation technique. The awkward and jerky movements of the two men in this film (due to the single-frame filming, which breaks down the continuum of motion by omitting transitional movements) help to convey the grotesque rituali-sation of man's inhumanity to man, and show the spectator a form of human gesture only possible with this type of photography. What concerns us here specifically, however, are those animated films in which the surrealist sensibility is most present—in films which are drawn and painted (not on the stock), which are of a fictional nature, and which attempt a realistic look; the work of the Disney factory being the ultimate example.

Fictional animation can either attempt to capture a realistic look or not. Some artists find the attempt useless because of the inherent limitations of the *genre* (the human hand could never compete with the camera in accurately rendering reality). These animators exploit the very uniqueness of the medium which allows them to dwell on minimal elements with varying degrees of stylisation. The epitome of this style of animation can be seen in much of the work coming from the studios of Eastern Europe since the Sixties, where fictional characters may move and speak and convey ideas, but are often represented as strangely-personified geometric shapes (the protagonist as cube or triangle), with voices of no human tongue, but of a more universal

language of "beep"'s and "squeak"'s. This non-realistic form of animation, with its feeling for sparseness, is more acceptable to the reality-
conscious spectator, who sees realistically-animated film as a "fail-
ure" ("Why draw it when photography can do it so much better?").

For the spectator who does not wish to avoid reality (as in the
above-mentioned films which reject reality from the start) but to transcend it, the realistic fictional animated film provides the ideal opportunity. These works are more cluttered (with the devices of realism; for
example, characters cast shadows) in their vision. The realistic
animator is the ultimate surrealist in his search for perfect images. No
other form of film-making offers the artist so much control over his
subjects and the devices of his technique as the animated film. Lighting
does not depend on the fickleness of the weather (the animator can
paint his sunlight where he wants it); physically impossible camera
movements can be accomplished with minimal effort in the animation
room; and even the specific gesture or expression of a character can be
completely regulated by the animator if he has only the time and talent.
The perfect mechanical aspects of the animated film provide the realistic animator with the ideal opportunity to crystallise his realistic vision, and at the same time to employ those effects that are *only* possible
with animation. In this way realistic animation is idealised and transforms itself into a kind of hyper-realism.

Within the basic realistic vision of this kind of film simultaneously
exists the absurdity of attempting the impossible. As hard as the
Disney artist may work at rendering perfectly synchronous lip movements to his singing bears, he can never really succeed in being "real."
(Bears just do not sing, anyway; at least not like humans; and the
personification of animals is another level of absurdity.) In this way a
schizophrenic vision is apparent, and the inherent duality of the
realistically-animated fictional film exists in the contrast between the
intensity of *ideally*-realised images and the obvious unreality of the
genre. This is a juxtaposition that is absent from those more abstract or
stylised animated films, which reject reality as their basic premise.

Before studying the work of Disney, where this type of film finds its
apogee, a look at the *Betty Boop* films of the early Thirties (created by
Max and Dave Fleischer, also the creators of *Popeye*) will reveal a
more consciously surreal sensibility, based less on the creation of
intense and idealised images, and more on the devices of distortion,
metamorphosis and exaggeration. (The M-G-M cartoons of Tex Avery
are another source of extreme exaggeration in animated film.)

Beneath the adventurous exteriors of the *Betty Boop* films is a world
of hallucinatory creepiness and lurid sexual innuendo, making these

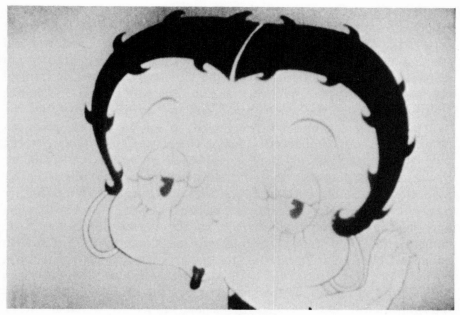

"Boop-oop-a-doop"

films as popular with adults as with children. When a male animal would demonstrate a desirous intention toward Miss Boop, it would not be uncommon for him to run his huge, hairy hands over her entire body, slurping and grunting lustfully. Miss Boop herself is the absurdist's sexpot: beneath her naive face and quivering body is the heart of a slut. Patterned on the "Boop-oop-a-doop" Girl of the Twenties (the double image of Helen Kane), Betty's body, if one takes a close look at it, is a completely accurate study of the female physique. It is the woman's head that is strange. Much too large for her petite but ripe form, Betty's head is a caricature of baby-faced innocence, with its naive round eyes, and tiny puckered lips. The body is so real—yet the head so unreal; and therein lies the absurdity of her character.

The visual style of these films is composed mostly of images of metamorphosis, distortion and exaggeration. All the characters are alive! Every figure in a *Betty Boop* film is filled with pulsating, throbbing life; even when standing still, we can fell them *breathing*, their bodies quivering like jelly, and we are made aware of the inner lives of these creatures. (This quivering quality appears in a recent short animated film by the National Film Board of Canada, *Walking*, where a different technique is used, but to similar effect, to show the various ways in which people carry themselves when walking.) From the bodies of these ever-pulsating figures new beings continually metamorphoze. In *Snow White*, the most obviously surreal of the series, the wicked witch's mirror is the device of transformation (though a device is not always needed, for a Fleischer character can transform itself at will). As Koko the clown performs a rhythmical strutting dance to the soundtrack of Cab Calloway's eerie "St. James Infirmary Blues," the witch flies in and waves her mirror over the clown, turning him into a flowing white phantom. As the phantom continues to move sensuously across the screen, the camera tracks with him into a "haunted house" sequence where the rear walls are decorated with paintings of distorted, shrieking faces; skulls and skeltons are piled in the dark recesses of the background. With another pass of the mirror the witch now transforms herself into a bat-like fish and flies circles around the clown, continually darting close to the camera's lens and then receding into the background. Koko then changes from a phantom into a strange, tubular-octopus shape, with elastic limbs that contort his body and enable him to tie himself into knots while still crooning the song and strutting along. As he straightens himself into an erect posture, his head immediately changes into a liquor bottle, and pours himself a drink from his head. As a sustained example of hallucinatory metamorphosis in animated film this sequence has hardly been surpassed.

Minnie the Moocher contains further examples of distortion and exaggeration. In this film Miss Boop wipes her mouth with a handkerchief at one point, only to leave her bright lips still singing by themselves on the cloth. (Buñuel is not the only one concerned with misplaced body parts.) Betty flaunts herself by forcefully thrusting herself into the lens. Her tiny body stays behind as her huge face looms into the lens, and her eyes and mouth protrude even further as she magnifies herself for the voyeuristic spectator.

The *Betty Boop* films have not lost their influence. Their hallucinatory visual nature and lurid sexual innuendo (enhanced by the black-white-grey coarseness of their tonalities) have been perpetuated in the Underground comics of today, especially in that style of raunchy decay portrayed by San Francisco illustrator R. Crumb.

Unlike the *Betty Boop* cartoons, the Disney animated films have no hidden "adult" level. They are films created for the childlike. Often

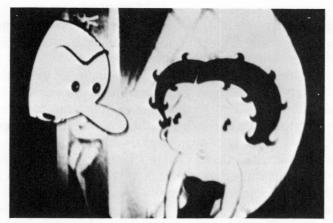

SNOW WHITE. The ugly witch sticks her head through her mirror...

...and in one second of film time...

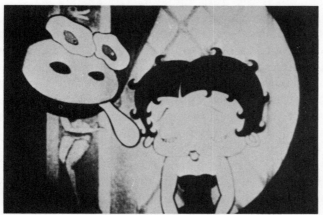

...her head is transformed into a frying-pan with two eggs

criticised for the naivety of their vision (a criticism coming only from "corrupted" adults; no children have as yet voiced any objections) which is an obvious and inherent feature of the childlike, the intensity and truth of the vision often goes unnoticed by the adult critic who has lost touch with that free element of his personality. The Disney films are as an intensely-felt reality as that of a child. It is a world of idealised images and archetypes; and to put oneself fully into a Disney film, without reservation, puts one into a world of completely unpretentious perception, where good is good, evil is evil, and red is red.

Within his fictionalised format Disney clutters as many elements as possible to make his films dense in realistic features. If the characters in a *Betty Boop* cartoon do much heavy breathing, the characters in a Disney film live a more relaxed life. Animals and figures move smoothly, with perfect lip synchronisation and shadows that follow them about. The complete animation of all twenty-four frames undoubtedly aids in controlling this hyper-realism. Human gesture is so extremely refined in the films (and to see an animal perform a human gesture so perfectly only heightens the absurdity) that movements are frequently balletic. In the "Dance of the Hours" sequence from *Fantasia* we actually find a parody of ballet, where huge hippos pose as ballerinas in lacey tutus and comport themselves with hilariously accurate gestures of gentility. Alligators play the villains, and in one shot lasting but a second, we see one of them preparing to make an attack on a hippo with the all panache of a silent movie villain, as he quickly strokes an imaginary moustache in demoniacal glee. The Disney character (whether human or personified animal) is the most completely drawn personality of the animated cinema.

One technical device that provides these films with their intensely "real" dimension is the tracking shot. The Disney artist delights in tracking, expecially through forests (*Bambi, Snow White and the Seven Dwarfs*), and to give his frames their added dimension of intense depth he continually changes the focus within his frames as objects (trees in this case) come nearer to the spectator's plane of vision. No other animator puts as much emphasis on this optical nature of his work. It is not a changing of focus that flows naturally from the dictates of his equipment (the animation camera never moves through space, so its focus is always constant) but one that is incorporated into the painting of the frames themselves, and gives an incredible simulation of the workings of the human eye by a totally artificial method.

In the pictorialisation of water, fire and lightning the Disney artistry gives an intense reality to the elements of nature as seen through childlike eyes. Usually found at crucial moments in the films, these

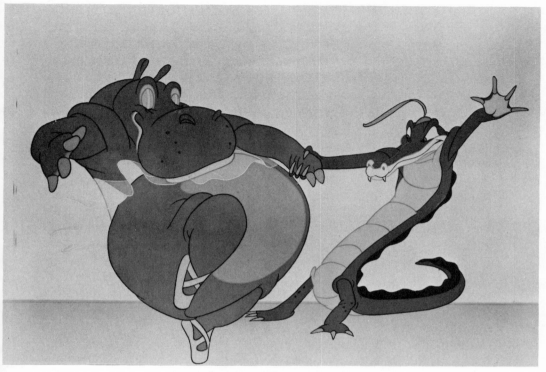

Human gestures caricaturised

natural occurrences are used as visual-emotional punctuation to the scenes. The purity of the forest setting in *Bambi* is enhanced by raindrops that glisten like diamonds (remember the tear-drop that changes into a diamond in Cocteau's *Beauty and the Beast*?) and roll rhythmically over leaves and vines to the "April Showers" song. Streams in a Disney films have a magical and changing consistency. In capturing fire, one of the most difficult things to show realistically, the Disney artist breaks down the colour into paint-by-number like areas of red, orange, yellow and white which, when seen in movement, combine to give an effect of intense heat. Lightning is probably Disney's favourite natural element (judging from the frequency with which it appears in his films). Storms become studies in black and white, where for split-seconds all the elements in the frames are illuminated by white highlights, and occasionally an entire frame will be pure white. By the use of opaque paints, the Disney artist gives a plastic quality to substances which in reality (water, fire and lightning) are so fleeting and transparent as to escape our perceptive scrutinisation.

Fantasia, though rich in intense images, is the least surreal of all the Disney features. This can be attributed to a few reasons. Firstly, the anthology structure of the film tends to break down the spectator's emotional involvement; but more importantly, the visualisation of concrete images to music, disdained by some people at the time as a pretentious attempt to popularise classical music, is far too structured a concept, limiting the creative capacity of the viewer by enforcing upon him specific "stories". If one does not conjure up images of angelic centaurs frolicking in idyllic landscapes when listening to Beethoven's "Pastoral" one is given no choice in the matter but to accept the Disney version. When abstract music is so concretely realised there is little room in which the mind can ramble. The Bach Fugue sequence (one of the few fully-realised American works of Oskar Fischinger, the German colourist-animator whose genius was stifled by Hollywood) seems to be an answer to this problem, where the mathematical music of Bach is set to abstract patterns that look like shooting stars and sky-writing *à la* Kandinsky. Though the most innovative sequence in the film, it is emotionally weak, and has the effect of a light show which one watches enchanted by the patterns but unaffected. For the emotional effect of pure colour in the animated film one must turn to Fischinger's German *Composition in Blue* and *Circle*.

It is in the films of sustained fiction that the intensity of Disney's vision predominates. *Bambi* and *Sleeping Beauty* show Disney at his most archetypal highpoint. Both films are illustrations of childhood mythology: the former, a serious study of the Odyssey theme; the latter, an idealised fairy tale of romantic illusion.

Of all the Disney films *Bambi* is one that has the most traumatic effect on its younger viewers, and in its intensity leaves its mark the longest by lingering in the minds of most adults who see it in their childhood. This impact is due to the fact that the film deals with the Odyssey theme—the primal search for self—and though Bambi does not actually travel anywhere in his search, by his attitude of constant enquiry into the mysteries of life which are so new to him, and his naive pursuit for truth, he is still the archetypal character in search of self-realisation. We see Bambi from birth to his entry into manhood where, having overcome a series of trials, tribulations and fears, he takes his place beside his father as leader of the pack.

Bambi is the Disney factory's most concentrated film of animal personification. The absence of a single human figure in the film, and the insular nature of the forest setting, help to bring out the humanity of the animals. They are warm, sensitive and aware creatures, who live their lives peacefully. They are endearing. One remembers Flower, the

skunk, who pops from some shrubbery with a halo of flowers encircling his quizzically-sniffing head; Bambi's mother, with her ever-maternally warm voice; Bambi's father, who by his silence and deliberate movements represents true majesty; and a sexy lady rabbit who flaunts her charms. Bambi himself still remains the most completely-developed character in a Disney film, and the attention to his personality which the studio showed can be seen in some of the layout boards of artists' renderings. One is called "The Adolescent Age" and depicts Bambi in various gestures and expressions, treating him in the same manner as a live actor. (The acutely human nature of the animals in this film may be in part due to the participation of Sidney Franklin, the producer-director of such "family" films—with *real* actors—as *The Good Earth* and *The Barretts of Wimpole Street*).

Motherhood is pictured as quaintly protective, and as a spring rain sends the forest animals scurrying about to take shelter under toadstools, various groups of mothers are seen with their young ones trailing behind (for example, Mother Quail and her brood).

Alternating with these scenes of warmth and security in a sylvan setting are scenes of horrific terror. Beside the idyllic forest is a wide open field of high grass. Through ominous music and dialogue it is established that the field is a place of danger, to be ventured into only with great caution. At one point Bambi hears a gunshot and asks his father what it was. The stag replies, "Man has come into the forest," and a further ominous note is struck. One day Bambi and his mother are in the field gathering food. Suddenly, the music is heard. The haunting voice of the mother cries out, "Run Bambi, Run!" As Bambi runs the pacing accelerates, and he leaps alone into the forest. A shot is heard. Bambi's father enters, and answers his son's frightened expression with a remorseful yet stern reply that "Man has taken your mother away." Fade out. The finality of the remark is unquestionable as Bambi and the spectator are confronted with this reality of life.

That man is made the villain of the film (and never actually shows his face) is the essence of the film's heaviness. The spectator is confronted not only with his own warm, spontaneous nature (as depicted by the animals in the film) but also with his cruel, destructive side (as em-

The womb-like warmth of the forest setting

Terror

bodied by "man"). In this way the work contains an undercurrent of paranoiac schizophrenia which no doubt accounts for much of the terror of the vision.

Later in the film a forest fire, spread by man, ravages the forest.

As Bambi matures he sprouts little horns and uses them in the climactic fight scene to attack a rival buck for the favours of a young doe. The fight is portrayed in stark shadows and with threatening music. It is the final ordeal through which Bambi must pass in order to reach maturity. He wins, and goes to take his place beside his father on a promontory high above the forest floor, as a choir sings a hopeful song and the camera tracks back through the verdant forest. Although the ending is optimistic and peaceful, the film has not been without its moments of primal terror.

Sleeping Beauty has none of the threatening quality of *Bambi*. The wicked witch and her crew of uglies may be horrific, but in a purely fantastical way. One remembers this film not for any richness of theme, so slight as it is, but for its intensely imagistic nature. Here we have the modern, streamlined Disney, with a look that is less cluttered

BAMBI

with the devices of realism than the earlier films (though it still could hardly be called sparse). The CinemaScope ratio is used, and zoom shots replace the older depth-tracking shots. The edges of the painted areas are sharper and less romantically hazy; and the painted areas themselves have less shading and detail. These areas of pure colour may be the influence of Colour Field painting which was just starting to develop in America. All these elements give the film its uniquely sharp, almost harsh, vision of a fairy tale which has usually been treated with more romantic lushness: from Perrault's original tale, through Doré's engravings, to Tchaikovsky's music and infinite ballet versions.

As a large story-book opens before our eyes we are let into the world of illusion. In the court scenes, the lords and ladies stand in highly-stylised groupings, tracing a sharp Renaissance perspective toward the background. When one of the three fairies makes a wish at a point in the film, her vision includes an extreme close-up of a moist, red rose. (One thinks of Magritte's "The Wrestler's Tomb," where a huge red rose takes up the space of a room.) And the final shot has the prince and princess dancing in the clouds in a shot remeniscent of the final scene in *Beauty and the Beast*.

Metamorphosis is gloriously present in the film. In order to destroy Sleeping Beauty, the witch changes herself into a green glow that hovers in the hallway of the castle, enticing Aurora into an almost slow-motion ascension up the stairs. At the film's climax the witch transforms herself into a flame-throwing dragon that lurches high above the protagonists; but the forces of good turn her arrows into flowers, and the boulders that come hurtling off cliffs into bubbles. Here we have a harmless vision. The story book closes.

7

The Artist-Inventor

"I am trying to make you *see!*"
—D. W. Griffith (to Lillian Gish)

"In the future everybody in the world will be world famous for fifteen minutes."
—Andy Warhol

In the minimal art of today the surrealist sensibility that was established in the early years of this century finds its contemporary fruition. Both minimal art and early surrealism are artistic visions that seek primarily to expand human consciousness on all levels. "Minimal" is not a derogatory word implying limited value or effect, but a word descriptive of the outward look of a work of art. A minimal art work is simply one in which the external elements (the gloss of elaboration) have been reduced to enable the truer internal life of the work to shine through. (The "black" canvasses of Ad Reinhardt are a good early example. At first sight they appear to be large black paintings; but on closer inspection one sees that they are made up of rectangular areas of slightly different shades of black, and one's first conception is shattered.) If abstract art arose in opposition to realism in order to provide an alternative to the photographic accuracy of the camera, and non-representational art developed in order to de-intellectualise the image of abstraction, then minimal art can be seen as a further refining of the image in order to emphasise its basic qualities (be they depth, space, texture, light, etc.). These qualities are perceived in conceptual revelations ("It's not just a black canvas after all!") and in this way manifest the surrealist viewpoint.

It is not surprising that most of the art of today is minimal on some level, for we live in an age of specialisation. The Renaissance man had his many talents; but today's artist can spend years exploring all the possible variations on one specific concept. (Jean Renoir has stated that all artists explore only one theme in their lifetime.)

Minimal art leaves the most room for the mind of the spectator to wander around, and in doing so shows itself to be a very respectful approach, placing a high importance on the interpretations of every viewer. Botticelli once remarked contemptuously that "by throwing a sponge soaked with different colours at a wall one can make a spot in which a beautiful landscape can be seen." Leonardo, one of his peers, scolded him for this hauty remark by stating that one can learn much from such smudges, and Botticelli, he said, was a painter of very bad landscapes. Piero Di Cosimo created magnificent equestrian battles and landscapes from studying the walls on which sick people would spit and vomit. The human mind can see the most spectacular visions in the least inspiring places, and this kind of perception is part of the greatness of the artist.

One can see the relationship between the Di Cosimo approach and the *frottage* method of Max Ernst, in which his hallucinatory faculties were stimulated by elements of his surroundings, enabling him to create works in a *passive* manner by letting the medium guide himself (rather than the other way around). As a base, Ernst would scrape pigment on a colour-prepared foundation which he would place on uneven surfaces. How much more immediate is this kind of approach, which brings the artist directly in contact with his environment, than the isolated ivory-tower method of the conventional landscape painter who sits with his easel aloof from the scene he is depicting. Ernst created a new kind of landscape, in which the actual texture of the environment is incorporated into the work of art itself. In film, the passivity of the artist can be seen in *Un chien andalou* where Dali and Buñuel claim they excluded any image which they found they could consciously interpret or give meaning to. They let the film medium guide *them,* and the editing technique based on relationships of form is a good example of this. Through the confrontation with the *environment* that this passive approach stresses, the spectator can more easily be brought out of his own insular world into a realisation of metaphysical awareness.

The conceptual nature of film has a tradition as long as film history itself. Even before the cinema as we know it was invented, Eadweard Muybridge had taken a series of pictures of a horse in movement which he later ran through an improvised projector, thereby analysing the nature of motion. Motion in film is based on the persistence of vision in the human eye. As one frame vanishes from the screen, its image is momentarily retained in the mind. With the continual build-up of twenty-four frames per second, and the corresponding persistence of these lingering images, motion is conveyed. In this way static shots, which neither move on the screen nor within the frames themselves,

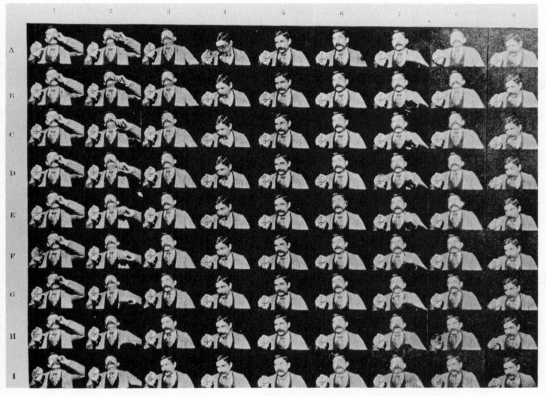

"Fred Ott's Sneeze." A one-shot film broken down into multiples

are given movement, and the mind of the spectator is tricked, thereby establishing all films within the context of *trompe-l'oeil*. The intensity of film's illusionary nature can be seen in the contemporary audience's reaction to the earliest Edison and Lumière shorts. A train would be shown in one simple shot chugging diagonally across the screen from the background to the foreground, making the spectators scream and run for cover, fearing the locomotive might run them over.

Revelation in minimal film can give new meaning to old things. Human gesture has been a continuing area of exploration. While Disney shows us man's grace in the hyper-realism of his animal's balletic gestures, the minimal film artist lets his camera sit back and take it all in with little additional comment. Edison's *The Kiss* (an elderly couple bill and coo for a period of time), in its way one of the most romantic films ever made, is an early example of minimal film, where a single action is not only extended (about one minute) but is made the entire subject matter of the film. *Fred Ott's Sneeze* is another early minimal film that shows an intensely perceptive vision of human gesture. Here the silliness of the action gives the film an absurd quality. To interpret these films merely as the work of technical experimenters would be short-sighted, for they are also the expressions of *explorers of perception*. The first film-makers were artists who sought to make their audience see new things. After the technical devices of the cinema had been perfected, the concept of revelation through experimentation disappeared (a notable exception being the work of Alexandre Alexeieff, who created visions by illuminating pins stuck through a screen at different levels — see *Une nuit sur le mont chauve);* it is only today that film-makers are re-exploring ways of perception through minimal means. These film-makers generally come from a background in the visual arts, which prepares them for their intensely-pointed way of looking at things.

Andy Warhol's first films were epic explorations of simple human gestures and events. *Sleep* shows a man sleeping for six hours (the film is really three hours of ten-minute sequences shown twice). *Kiss* and *Blow Job* are self-explanatory. Warhol, in these lengthy films, carries Edison's technique to its ultimate conclusion. In the minimal film elements of structure are *stretched* to extreme exaggeration in order to expand the internal meanings of the works. David Rimmer, an experimental film-maker working today, deals sometimes in loop-films, where a single gesture or moment is seen over and over again. His *Dance* has a crazy absurdity as he loops a shot of a couple dancing around a ballroom floor (old stock footage). Through the repetition of this image a seemingly unimportant action is emphasised and elevated to a level of importance. Elongation, repetition and the shattering of conditioned expectations play a major part in the minimal sensibility. René Clair's *Entr'acte* contains a scene that can be seen as a precursor to the Rimmer film. Here we witness a robust washer-woman carrying her load of laundry up a stairway. Just as she is about to reach the top step she finds herself (through a jump cut) at the bottom again, and continues to mount the stairway. This action is repeated innumerable times for absurd effect, the absurdity coming less from the symbolic meaning of the sequence (failed orgasm) than from the very contrast between the seemingly ordinary action and the importance that it is given.

Minimalism is more predominant in non-fictional, experimental film than in fictional film, for the need to create a realism (on some level) in the latter necessitates much icing on the cake. The fictional film is inherently too cluttered with the devices of realism and theatricality to permit a good minimal feeling. The feature work of Walerian Borowczyk, however, is a rare exception of minimal fictional film; his *Goto, ile d'amour* and *Blanche* have the barren and ritualised quality of a production of *Waiting for Godot*.

The most metaphysical of all minimal film-makers is Michael Snow, who only started on a regular (if sporadic) basis in 1964 after many years as a painter-sculptor. In the first half of the Sixties Snow concentrated on his *Walking Woman* series. Here he explored all the possible variations on one theme: the profile silhouette of a contemporary woman (dressed in a knee-length skirt) caught in the midst of a stride. With this as his basic form, Snow created walking women in wood, plaster, metals, on canvas, stencilled her on walls, and placed her in landscapes (at Expo '67). In 1966/7 he made his first major film, *Wavelength,* a film which demands nothing of its audience but that they give the film their complete attention. Its meaning can only be revealed in the dialogue that occurs between viewer and film. *Wavelength* is a forty-five-minute slow zoom from one end of the artist's eighty-foot studio in New York to the other. Here we see a long room with four windows at the far end. In front of the windows are a desk with a telephone, two chairs, some radiators, and three pictures tacked on the wall. At the start a woman enters to supervise the moving of a bookcase. After she has left the zoom starts imperceptibly, and only the occasional jiggle of the camera breaks this "invisible" movement. As the film progresses three other human intrusions into the frame occur: the woman returns and listens briefly to the radio (The Beatles are singing "*Strawberry Fields:*" "Nothing is real. . .living is easy with eyes closed, misunderstanding all you see"); later a man enters and collapses (he is mostly obscured from our vision as the zoom has by this point cut down the area of the studio covered in the frame); and later still the woman returns to find the body (which we do not see at all), phones someone to report the death, and leaves.

The zoom continues. The object of the zoom's inquisition is one of the pictures tacked on the wall (a black-and-white photograph of waves rolling in to a shore). Gradually, the screen is filled with the area of the photo; and eventually, the zoom continues further into the photo itself and then stops. It starts to zoom slowly out, but only momentarily, as the frame blurs to white, followed by the pure white of the projector's lamp light on the screen, and the film is over. In addition to the background sounds (the dialogue of the four "theatrical" sequences and the noise of distant traffic in the street below) there is a sine wave which increases from fifty cycles per second to 12,000 cps with an excrutiatingly satisfying intensity over a period of forty minutes. As barren of frills as the film seems, there are some additional touches. It

is not filmed over a continuous forty-five minutes, thereby enabling day and night shots, different light sources, and filters for different colour effects. Also, at one point late in the film, there occurs a kind of flashback to a moment a few minutes earlier, and a superimposition can be seen until the zoom in the flashback sequence has caught up with the position of the zoom as we left it, and then the double exposure disappears as the zoom continues.

Wavelength is a film of most intense audience confrontation. Its structure is that of a crescendo, and except for the brief flashback, it propels the spectator continually and relentlessly forward both by its movement across the space of the studio and by its ever-amplifying soundtrack. It is a film of tremendous impetus, which challenges the viewer to look for himself, to discover what is there.

What *is* there? As the film progresses new elements continually arise that were previously not visible. At the film's start we can see the windows and barely what is outside them. We content ourselves with this; but as the zoom progresses, gradually cutting out the peripheral elements from our vision, we search for something more. As the windows come closer to our plane of vision we can see the street outside, the windows of stores, the roofs of trucks passing by. Still further into the film we can read the lettering on those awnings and shop front windows across the street. We are always finding new things to study. Continually our expectations are being shattered. This barren room which the (impatient) viewer thinks he knows, continually reveals more things where new revelations were thought impossible.

Not only does *Wavelength* continually reveal new things to the spectator, but it constantly raises questions in the mind of the viewer. The first and most obvious question one has is about the final object that the zoom will come to rest upon (once one has realised that this lengthy zoom will have to come to rest on something eventually). What is it going to be? At the start of the film the wall is too far away for us to figure out what it will be; but as the film progresses each viewer realises *at his own special moment* (and that is why this is such an open and respectful film) what that object is (the photograph); again, each viewer perceives the *nature* of the photo (waves) at his own individual time. In this way the film is a constant voyage of personal discovery.

Anything is possible in *Wavelength*. Just because this film is composed of a lengthy zoom forward, it does not exclude the possibility of another movement (and the flashback shows us there can be a diversion). Are there any freeze frames? So slow and imperceptible is the zooming movement that the entire film seems like a series of slightly-changing still frames; yet we *know* there is movement (seen more in retrospect, looking at the ground that has been covered), and the thought that there might be a *real* freeze frame in the film (something Snow, in his meticulous manner, probably did not overlook) strikes one with amazing absurdity.

Besides altering our awareness of movement, the film also changes our perception of time. Being confronted with such minimal material increases the intensity of our concentration and we lose ourselves in the time of the film. It may be forty-five minutes long but so much happens (depending on how involved one is in the film and how much one sees) that it seems longer. It becomes timeless.

The relationships that one sees in this work are rooted purely in the elements of film. At the moment one realises that it is the bottom of the three pictures to which the camera is zooming, one perceives the formal relationship between the dimensions of the screen and the dimensions of the picture — they are rectangles whose sides are of identical ratio. In one's mind a pleasing formal picture is ocurring, where one can see how the smaller rectangle will eventually grow until it fills the space presently occupied by the bigger rectangle of the screen; and geometry is thus given an emotional interpretation.

Snow has said, "My film is closer to Vermeer than to Cézanne." This leads one to believe that for him the structural relationships are less important than those based on light. At one point in the film when the frame is filled with part of a window, its moulding, and the wall with the pictures on it, Snow cuts from the scene depicted in daylight to the scene at night. It is a brilliantly shocking moment, in which the entire *look* of the film changes. From the soft golden hues of daylight to the cold bluish tones of artificial light we are immediately confronted with two opposite realities (day and night). If the precise arrangement and clear sunlight of the day shot remind one of Vermeer, the cold clarity, rectilinear elements and limited but intense colour of the night shot make one think of Mondrian.

Another relationship exists in the contrast between the film's tight structure (it is so obviously a planned film and has nothing of improvisation about it) and the open freedom with which one approaches viewing it. As structured as the film may be, there is no structuring of the spectator's emotional response to it, and it is truly, as Buñuel has stated regarding his own work, a film from which the spectator can take what is most useful .

In *Wavelength* Snow takes us from a room to the sea, and ends with us floating in white, open space. In *La région centrale* (1970/71) he puts us on land and then transports us into space and beyond. It is a film that uses a technique that has never been attempted before or since, and thereby exists as a totally autonomous work; yet in its very uniqueness and totality it encompasses all art and reflects upon man's place in the universe. This universal quality comes from the landscape nature of the film. This is not only a three-hour film which depicts a certain terrain, but also, because of its unique way of looking at that land, makes the spectator confront certain questions regarding his place in relation to that land. It is a transcendental film that takes the spectator on a trip, not only above the earth's surface, but above and beyond himself.

Snow has set his camera in the middle of an isolated, almost primeval, rugged mountainous landscape in northern Québec. The natural elements of the film are rocks, boulders, scrub brush, distant, tree-covered hill tops, a sliver-thin finger lake, and of course sky and clouds. Being autumn, the colours are rich umbers, siennas, dulcet greens and golds. The camera is mounted on a specially-built "tripod" which is a complex computer-programmed device that enables the camera to pan in literally *any* direction and at *any* angle. While hiding

LA REGION CENTRALE. The unique contraption in its isolated landscape

himself in a nearby valley, Snow let the contraption film the landscape
according to the various movements he had programmed into it. Not
only does this machine enable completely continuous horizontal pans,
but also verticle ones; and the camera can also be raised off the ground
and spun on its own axis. The combination of these movements (along
with zooming and focus changes) enables an infinite variety of motion.

Although the work is three hours long, Snow has said of it, "I'm not
interested in: 'It's three hours long but it seems like thirty minutes.'
I'm interested in: 'It's three hours long but it seems like 30,000 years.''
As its title implies, this is a film about the very core of being; the
essence of life. Through camera movements which have never been
seen before (panning back and forth, up and down; spinning right-side
up, upside-down; swooping and flying in ferris-wheel fashion) the

earth is shown to us in a completely fresh manner, and by the subjective nature of the film our identification is so extreme that we are forced to reflect upon our relationship with this "new land." For three hours *we are the camera,* perceiving the landscape in a completely subjective way (except for a brief moment near the beginning where the contraption's shadow is seen on the ground). There is nothing in the film to identify with but our own perceptions.

The work is composed of fourteen "symphonic" movements or sequences. Before each section a white "X" appears across the black screen (a simulated Academy Leader effect) to mark the start of a new camera movement. The passages of movements (they are all pans) range from thirty seconds in length to about twenty minutes, and the speeds of the motions vary from extremely slow (where it takes a few minutes to reveal a few feet of earth) to dizzingly speedy (where 360 degrees flash by in half a second). In the course of the fourteen movements we go through a day, from dawn to dusk, night, and the following day. The soundtrack consists of three electronic sounds (a hum, a ringing noise and a wining sound) which vary in frequency, rhythm and intensity throughout the film, according to the speed of the camera's movements. Any more literal description of the film beyond this would be confusing due to the minimal nature of what is actually up on the screen. The true meaning of the film can only be established between each spectator and the film; but some of the things it shows us and some of the questions it raises *can* be expressed.

La région central reveals the history of art
space movement colour form
are its preoccupations
(yet only some)
the screen becomes a moving colour field painting

after a lengthy period panning just the earth
the camera lifts up to the sky and pans just the sky
we have gone from being "*in* brown" to being "*in* blue"
colour is absorbed into us

near the end as the movements flash past the earth
earth tones are blurred but evocative
think of the landscapes that recede into a work of
piero della francesca
think of the cave paintings of lascaux
where paleolithic deer and cattle convey in rich earth tones
a similar sense of life and rushed movement and urgency
think of the freedom of movement in a work by jackson pollock

A four-second sequence: camera rotates simultaneously with horizontal movement; the earth appears to be spinning

La région centrale reveals the nature of optics
the science of sight

as the camera floats through space it turns on its axis
the impression given is that of the earth actually spinning
before our eyes
we all *know* the earth is spinning
while we stand with our feet firmly planted on it
but who has actually *seen* it
spin?

at one moment we are spinning clockwise
sequence ends
white "X" on black
the "X" appears to be turning counter-clockwise
an optical illusion

as the earth spins we see a *continuous* horizon line
not the linear horizon into which the western hero rides
but the circular, endless horizonless horizon of the east

La région centrale reveals our place in the universe
it is an empty landscape . . . but we are in it

if the man of fifteen hundred saw the land
through the frame of his chapel window
a window on the world
where miniature landscapes recede in deep perspective
the man of two thousand sees the land
in himself
and himself *in* the land

the camera pans the sky for a long time
no sight of land
there are no clouds
no sight of movement
losing sight of space and time
we are lost in the sky
we are *just there* in a moment of stasis
yet we know we (the camera) are still travelling through space

and what of the moon?
our closest neighbour in space
we tend to magnify its importance in our universe
here it is set right
the screen is black when suddenly
a tiny white ball darts into frame
(it's the moon! one realises)
the camera's movement bounces the ball
back and forth
off the four sides of the screen
like a ping-pong ball
(or a darting sperm?)
there is no romance to this moon
no ethereally floating clouds that mask its presence
no sitting lovers in a hollywood film

La région centrale's final sequence (number fourteen):

zooming while panning
faster the earth spins
sounds increase
we are coming to a climax
earth-sky-earth-sky-earth-sky-earth-sky
brown-blue-brown-blue-brown-blue-brown-blue
yet within the brown separate movements can be seen:
lines streak by
vertically
diagonally
horizontally
the movement slows gradually
we see rocks in the brown
we see sky in the blue
the finite earth
the infinite sky
the sun appears and whitens the. sky
white on white
a second sun appears (lens diffractions?)
two whites merge slowly
pure white
orange flashes momentarily on the screen
an "X" appears slightly orange (with spray paint?)
the end.

where is our place
in relation
to earth
and sky
?

Selected Bibliography

Some of this literature has been mentioned in the text; and some of it hasn't. It is all good reading.

ACCONCI, Vito, in *Avalanche*, Fall 1972.
BAUDELAIRE, Charles, *Artificial Paradise*, Herder and Herder,1971.
BRETON, André, *Nadja*, Grove Press, 1960.
BROWNLOW, Kevin, *The Parade's Gone By . . .*, Alfred A. Knopf, 1968.
BUÑUEL, Luis, *L'age d'or and Un chien andalou*, Lorrimer, 1968.
BURROUGHS, Williams, *Last Words of Dutch Schultz*, Cape Goliard.
CABANNE, Pierre, *Dialogues with Marcel Duchamp*, Thames and Hudson, 1971.
CAPRA, Frank, *The Name Above the Title*, Macmillan, 1971.
CHAPLIN, Charles, *My Autobiography*, Simon and Schuster, 1964.
COCTEAU, Jean, *Opium*, Peter Owen, 1957.
DALI, Salvador, *Les Díners de Gala*, Felicie Inc., 1973.
DURGNAT, Raymond, *Films and Feelings*, Faber and Faber, 1967.
DURGNAT, Raymond, *Luis Buñuel*, Movie Magazine, 1967.
EISNER, Lotte, *The Haunted Screen*, University of California Press, 1969.
ERNST, Max, *La Femme 100 têtes*, Gerhardt Verlag, 1962.
FINCH, Christopher, *The Art of Walt Disney*, H. N. Abrams, 1973.
FRANKENSTEIN, Alfred, *The Reality of Appearance*, New York Graphic Society, 1970.
FULLER, Samuel, *144 Piccadilly*, Richard W. Baron, 1971.
HAMMOND, Paul, *Fragments of the Marvelous*, in *Art and Artists*, July 1973.
HUYSMANS, Joris-Karl, *Against Nature*, Penguin, 1959.
JULLIAN, Philippe, *The Symbolists*, Phaidon Press, 1973.
KYROU, Ado, *Le Surréalisme au Cinéma*, Le Terrain Vague, 1963.
LEIDER, Philip, editor of *Surrealism*, in *Artforum*, September 1966.
LIPPARD, Lucy R., *Surrealists on Art*, Prentice-Hall, 1970.
LOCKE, John, *Michael Snow's "La Région Centrale"*, in *Artforum*, November and December 1973.
MALRAUX, André, *Museum without Walls*, Doubleday, 1967.
McSHINE, Kynaston L., editor of *Information*, The Museum of Modern Art, 1970.
MEDJUCK, Joe, *The Life and Times of Michael Snow*, in *Take One*, Vol. 3 No. 3, April 1972.
MILLER, Henry, *The Time of the Assassins*, New Directions, 1962.
PELLICER, A. Cirici, *1900 en Barcelona*, Ediciones Polígrafa, 1967.

RAINER, Yvonne, *The Performer as a Persona*, in *Avalanche*, Summer 1972.

SALA, Carlo, *Max Ernst et la Démarche Onirique*, Editions Klincksieck, 1970.

SITNEY, P. Adams, *Film Culture Reader*, Praeger, 1970.

SITNEY, P. Adams, *Visionary Film*, New York Oxford University Press, 1974.

SNOW, Michael, *A Survey*, Art Gallery of Ontario, 1970.

SONTAG, Susan, *Against Interpretation*, Farrar, Straus and Giroux, 1966.

SPIES, Werner, *Max Ernst Frottages*, Thames and Hudson, 1969.

STEIN, Gertrude, *Ida*, Random House, 1941.

TRUFFAUT, François, *Hitchcock*, Simon and Schuster, 1967.

TYLER, Parker, *Magic and Myth of the Movies*, Simon and Schuster, 1947.

VIVA, *Superstar*, G. P. Putnam's Sons, 1970.

VON STERNBERG, Josef, *Fun in a Chinese Laundry*, Macmillan, 1965.

WALDBERG, Patrick, *René Magritte*, André de Rache, 1965.

WEINBERG, Herman G., *"A Woman of Paris" in 1973*, in *Take One*, Vol. 3 No. 9 May 1973.

WEINBERG, Herman G., *The Complete Greed of Erich von Stroheim*, Arno Press, 1972.

WEINBERG, Herman G., *Josef von Sternberg*, E. P. Dutton, 1967.

WHITMAN, Walt, *Leaves of Grass* (first edition), Viking Press, 1959.

WILHELM, Richard, *The I Ching*, Bollingen Foundation, 1967.

WOOD, Robin, *Hitchcock's Films*, Zwemmer/Barnes, 1969.

YOUNGBLOOD, Gene, *Expanded Cinema*, Dutton, 1970.

Indexes

167

INDEX OF ART WORK